DOCTOR! DOCTOR!

DOCTOR! DOCTOR!

Tales of an Irish Practice

Hugh and Alice Alport

ISIS
LARGE PRINT
Oxford

First published in Great Britain 2007
by
The Book Guild Ltd.

Published in Large Print 2009 by ISIS Publishing Ltd.,
7 Centremead, Osney Mead, Oxford OX2 0ES
by arrangement with
The Book Guild Ltd.

British Library Cataloguing in Publication Data
Alport, Hugh
   Doctor! Doctor!: tales of an Irish practice.
   – Large print ed.
   (Isis reminiscence series)
   1. Alport, Hugh – Anecdotes
   2. Alport, Alice – Anecdotes
   3. Obstetricians – Northern Ireland and Ireland
   – Ulster – Anecdotes
   4. Physicians (General practice) – Northern Ireland
   and Ireland – Ulster – Anecdotes
   5. Physician and patient – Northern Ireland and
   Ireland – Ulster – Anecdotes
   6. Large type books
   I. Title II. Alport, Alice
   610.9'22'416

ISBN 978–0–7531–9528–4 (hb)
ISBN 978–0–7531–9529–1 (pb)

Printed and bound in Great Britain by
T. J. International Ltd., Padstow, Cornwall

To Chris

Fellow student, doctor, rambler:
Best Man, Godfather to at least one of our children
. . . and the one who got us into all this in the first
place.

CONTENTS

These tales arise from a joint experience of nearly forty years in medical practice in the area: the hospital-based stories are Hugh's while the general practice ones are from both. Where the context doesn't make it clear who's speaking, then it doesn't matter, as it could have happened to either of us.

Prelude

We all have Defining Moments in our lives — those times you look back to and say, "My life was different after that." Mine came one idyllic spring evening in West Donegal. Chris and I, on our meandering way from Dublin to Belfast after an unbelievably hectic month of practical Obstetrics, had taken a short after-dinner stroll out of the village of Glenties. The sun still reflected off the brilliant white cottages as we looked down on them from the rise in the road, while the faint blue mist (and rather less faint odour) of turf smoke hung over the few streets that made up most of the village.

It was the sort of image that, with varying grades of tweeness, can be found on any of the legions of calendars of "Ould Ireland", sent out every year to warm the hearts of the proxy-Irish worldwide. But it was real and there before me; the epitome of peace and silent tranquillity. We'd been motor-cycling all day; perhaps the dinner, the wine and a couple of noggins of spirits afterwards had made me mellow. I knew — almost audibly I vowed — that I would be back. That much I knew — I did not know that I would spend my life there, in that extraordinary, wonderful, loveable, maddening island they call Ireland.

CHAPTER
ONE

Dublin

It all began with a casual query from Chris as we ambled, together with the rest of our Fifth-Year student class, into the morning Gynae lecture early in the Spring term: "Are you joining the Dublin party for Easter? There's a good few've signed up for it already, so think about it soon. I feel it could be good fun if enough of us go."

I didn't want to betray the fact that this was the first I'd heard of such a venture, living as I did a life of innocent seclusion outside the constraints of the timetable; I'd obviously missed some significant item of intelligence: it needed the roundabout approach.

"What d'ye reckon it'll involve, then — have you heard from anyone who's been?" (By this time I was already suspecting that this was an annual event so felt a shot in the near-dark was worthwhile.)

"Only two or three from last year — seems they had a whale of a time — very, er — different, apparently."

"Different?"

"Mmmm — 'Wild' was one of the descriptions, if I recall."

"What are we supposed to do, officially that is?"

"Get in our twelve normal deliveries and join in the teaching programme"

"And that's supposed to be Wild?"

"Ah, but you don't know Dublin." (This was where Chris had the advantage — he had Irish blood in his veins and considered it one of his minor claims to fame that one of his aunts had had a leg shot off by a shell from the British frigate that came up the Liffey to fire on the Four Courts during the 1916 Rising: the fact that she was an uninvolved non-combatant sitting on a window ledge watching the action wasn't allowed to get in the way of a good story. Yes, the Irish blood may have been dilute but it still ran thick enough to tell a tale.)

Thus it was that we came to pass an uncomfortable night on the cattle ferry to Belfast, which we followed with a motorcycle journey to Dublin in sheeting rain: hardly surprising, then, that we missed our planned arrival time by several hours.

We presented ourselves at the reception desk.

"Ah, 'tis yourselves, then?" said the duty porter, taking in, but too polite to comment on, our filthy, bedraggled state. "Dr Riley's been looking for you for ages — I'll tell him you're here." He waved aside my stammered attempts at an apology and picked up the phone.

Two minutes later, a white-coated young man breezed along, took a look at the apparitions before him, and said, "What the Hell's been keeping you two? I've a drip needs watching, so you'd better come with me." He was looking straight at me and I didn't feel

4

disposed to argue: maybe this was how they did things down here. I followed him, making one half of a singularly ill-matched duo — he with his smart white coat and stethoscope flying behind him; me trudging behind clumsily, still clad in full motorcycle gear and carrying in one hand a crash helmet and in the other a holdall, all leaving their own separate streams of water on the corridor behind me.

As we progressed in this way it was explained to me that I was to supervise an induction of labour by means of an Oxytocin drip. This involved recording the frequency and duration of contractions: once they reached the preordained levels, I was to report to my new mentor.

We entered a side-room where a woman lay in bed. Until then I imagine her time had been one of calm reflection on her impending motherhood; she turned in the bed as I entered and her gaze fell upon me. I'd never had the sort of effect on any woman that I had upon her in that instant — she turned pale, her eyes, dark against the acute pallor, bulged and her pupils widened. Her attempt to take a deep breath prior to a mighty scream was cut short by a contraction obviously of a different order of magnitude from those that had gone before.

"H — hello," I said. In the circumstances I couldn't even elaborate on this: I was too overcome by the thought that she was going to drop the child here and now, in front of a novice student (my "mentor" had hurtled off to carry out his mission of healing somewhere else, without so much as introducing us).

The contraction passed off in due course, however, as these things do, and I began to peel myself out of my wet things. My patient, now comfortable again, watched wide-eyed and open-mouthed as I stripped down to a merely damp jacket and trousers, ran a hand across my hair and settled into my best bedside professional attitude. She lay on the bed, not moving but seemingly unable to take her eyes off me. I tried to make conversation but she was evidently having some ongoing discomfort, for every few seconds her face distorted into a grimace and her neck muscles twitched.

"Would you like me to get you something for the pain? I can see you're having a bit of trouble between the contractions," I said, in my best Caring Voice.

That was the last straw — control, so bravely kept up, was wholly lost now. She started to laugh and once started was quite unable to stop. Her pallor gone, she was bright scarlet and had fallen back on the pillow, trying to get herself back under control.

"Ah, Doctor dear, I'm so sorry, but — well, you see, it's — well — have you had a look in a mirror since you came in?" (She was a good bit older than I was and probably had some maternal feelings to spare at the time; as well as that, she had already sussed me out sufficiently to see that I was probably in need of some of them — bless her.)

I took the hint and over to the mirror. I should have done this before ever allowing myself to be dragged off to meet strangers, even (or especially) patients. The image in the glass, unkempt and still damp around the collar, was of a near-black face from a hundred miles of road dirt, except around the eyes, where the goggles had left my natural (well, most of my natural) skin colour visible. I looked like nothing so much as a badly developed negative of a panda. No doubt my half-shuffling gait as I entered had only added to the startling apparition . . .

So there we were, she with the giggles, interrupted only by her contractions (quite normal and still mild, again), me inclined to join her as I tried to remove at least some of the road dirt with a paper towel, an effort which only provoked more hysterics from us both. After a bit I gave up and we settled down to talk about sensible things. After an hour of this we were almost old friends, so much so that when my relief came along we parted with genuine regret on my part and, I like to think, on hers also.

I got brief directions to the Residents' quarters from my successor, gathered up all the kit I'd shed on entering and found two problems straight off; first, I couldn't carry everything and once outside the room dropped it all in a heap to sort myself out. The only way I could carry my crash helmet was to stick it on my head, where it sat at a hopelessly oblique angle, still dripping water down my neck. The other problem was that while sitting warm and comfortable in the room, I hadn't noticed that water had penetrated to areas more intimate than the back of my neck; stepping out into the relatively cool corridor made me aware of the large chilly soaking area around my crotch and a glance down confirmed a very visible dark stain just where it was most liable to misinterpretation. I squelched off down the corridor to the Residence with all the aplomb of a seriously incontinent drunk, the impression no doubt reinforced by the way I was keeping my legs apart to stop the cold wet bits from chafing each other. I hoped to goodness no one would come through the corridor until I was safely out of it.

It was now past midnight; I'd had nothing to eat, hadn't seen any of my friends, was tired and filthy and needed nothing so much as a wash and a decent night's sleep. By any standards I should have been annoyed at the way I had been treated. But I wasn't; I was almost elated — I had been chucked in at the deep end and come up smiling, had met one charming lady (I didn't see her again; I hope all went well for her — she'd have made a smashing mother) and perhaps, just perhaps, had done some good in however unorthodox a way. If this was Ireland then Chris was right — it *was* different.

A few days into the routine, if the provision of First World obstetric services with a Third World workload can ever descend to "routine", we were grouped into threes to form the Flying Squad, God help us! Our task was to be the first (and wholly incompetent) responders to emergency calls from patients on our books who were threatening to miscarry. We sallied out by bus, taxi, bicycle, or, for one lucky trio, a battered old Austin, armed with six phenobarbitone tablets and a threepenny bit. If on arrival all seemed reasonable, the phenobarb. was handed out: "Just rest up for a day or two and take these, two three times a day, then we'll call and see you tomorrrow," said with our most reassuring manner, hoping that no one would see our firmly crossed fingers. We always left with the words: "If it gets any worse, do ring in again." At least it made us feel better. If things looked bad enough to need intervention, a sprint to the nearest phone box (nobody had private phones in those parts of Dublin then) saw the threepenny bit come into its own as we rang back to base to get a proper doctor. This was usually one of the more senior resident staff, who not only brought his skills to the house but drove the ambulance as well. Drink being the curse of the working classes, the chances were the doctor/driver would be well over the limit — if a limit had existed: but then it would have taken an awful lot for the Gardai to stop a speeding ambulance, however driven.

We learned the legends of the place, all of them with a foundation in fact, however dubious. We learned, for example, of the Resident-on-Call who not only had a degree of alcoholism that today would have seen him referred for treatment before being allowed to work at all, but who in addition had never driven a vehicle in his life (Driving Tests in Ireland were still in the future then). This was not considered a significant handicap, but the story goes that bills for bodywork repairs were getting out of hand by the time he moved on.

A parallel squad existed for Obstetric emergencies, to deal with the complications of late pregnancy and labour. This I managed to avoid, so I could never find myself in the sort of situation handed down in the folklore of the place, when a student rang in to base,

9

late at night, to wake up the On-Call Resident in a state of high alarm.

"H — h — how do you deal with a neck presentation?"

"Don't be bloody stupid, you can't have a neck presentation."

"Y — Y — yes you can — I've got the head here in my pocket!"

Apocryphal . . . ?

One of these visits stands out as a real frightener. The call came to a top-floor tenement dwelling close to the city centre. "It's the wife — I think she's having a miss." No cause for alarm there then: "Right, we'll be along."

The address took us in through a door that had long been a stranger to a lick of paint; opening it revealed a stair with a rather tatty carpet, which, it turned out, lasted only to the first landing. As we climbed, the stairs became more and more ramshackle until, on the last lap to the top, they were positively dangerous and in the dark would probably have seen us breaking something by going through any of the large gaps in the treads. The flat was silent — even then I knew that this usually meant trouble. The husband opened the door to us before we could knock and one look at him told us our instinct was right. He led us without ceremony through a living room devoid of any of the comforts and most of the necessities of decent living into an equally spartan bedroom which fulfilled its definition by containing a double bed, though precious little else.

On the bed, as white as the none-too-white sheets that covered her, was our patient, too weak to speak and almost too weak to register our arrival. Taking a history was a non-starter, so we gently pulled back the sheets. The bed was full of blood, the aborted foetus lying in the midst of the pool. There was no doubt about this one: this was a threepenny-bit job.

"Where's the nearest phone?" I asked the husband, who was now even more frightened than he had been before.

"I'll take you down — will she be all right, do you think now, Doctor?" I didn't dare answer as we negotiated the treacherous stairs again, this time at almost literally breakneck speed. The scruffy little shop next door had a phone — probably the only one for tens of yards on either side, but it was working and I was able to summon up the on-call Resident.

"OK, I'll bring the wagon along right away." Words of reassurance indeed.

"The stair's in a bloody awful state: we'll have bother getting her out on a stretcher, mind."

"Ach, don't worry about that," came the reply. "We'll sort her out." His voice was slurred — the Morning After was extending well into the afternoon.

(Well, it was his responsibility — he should have had plenty of experience of humping sick women down tenement staircases.)

The wagon was with us in commendably short order: even when pissed, he'd managed to find his way at high speed without hitting anything of significance and had

11

parked as tidily as you could wish of anyone, on the main road opposite the door.

One look was all he needed to agree with us: "We'll scrape her, so."

I offered to go for the stretcher. "Not at all, sure we'll just do it here."

We all protested our inability to administer a general anaesthetic here (or anywhere else, for that matter).

"Sure, in her state she's not going to need anything like that," came the confident dismissal of our concerns. Our concerns were not one bit dismissed by this; it conjured up visions of pre-anaesthetic surgery, of the three of us holding this poor creature down, if indeed she had the strength to struggle. However, presumably this was the way it was done here, so who were we to make a fuss?

Instruments and drugs were brought up and two of us found employment as stirrups and drip stands, one arm holding the bottle of saline high in the air while the patient's knee rested on the opposite shoulder. A dose of pethidine that even then I wouldn't have given to a horse ensured that she was either unconscious or in no state to object as she was curetted there and then — with considerable skill and expedition, I might say, considering the circumstances.

The procedure over and three or four pints of saline in her veins, our man rolled her back onto the now-replaced bed sheets, slapped her on the arm and said: "That'll do her well, so." As we left, I fielded an anxious beseeching look from the husband who made his appearance at the door as we trooped past. He said nothing. "We've done what we can," was all I could bring myself to say, "and we'll be back in the morning to see how she's doing." I couldn't say, "To see if she's still alive," although that was the unspoken sentiment.

She was, of course, on our list for follow-up visit the next day, though none of us was in any way keen to intrude on what would surely be a house of mourning. As it happened, the rooms overlooked the river and so wary were we of the situation that we crossed to the opposite side of the river to see if the curtains were drawn. Only when we'd located the windows did we recall that there were no curtains that would have been worth drawing anyway. There was nothing for it but to go on up.

A few steps from the top of the last flight, the door was flung open and we were greeted with a broad smile by a beaming, positively bouncing man, almost unrecognisable as the drawn strained fellow of the day before. It would be an understatement to say that we were heartened by this, but there was still an element of caution in our question: "How are things today, then?"

"Ah, she's fine now, just fine, Doctor — just like you said." We'd said nothing of the sort, but it looked as if the dice were rolling our way and who were we to complain?

He ushered us through into the bedroom, where our moribund victim of the day before was sitting up in bed, with an empty tray on the chair beside it bearing witness to a fully polished-off breakfast — probably a more generous one than she would ever see on a normal day. She was pale but smiling and overall in a remarkable state, considering how she had been barely eighteen hours beforehand. After the clinical formalities, we made our way out, quite prepared to take the credit for having wrought this particular miracle on our own. As we left, our man caught me by the arm and pressed into my hand a miniature bottle of Irish whiskey, thus unwittingly doing me a very bad turn — it gave me a taste for the stuff which persists undiminished to this day.

The obstetric side of the business was, at least for me, conducted entirely in-house, saving me and my patients from the consequences of incompetence away from base. Collecting normal deliveries was just a matter of waiting and grabbing the opportunities as they came along, competing with the other students (both my own group and those from the city's medical schools) and the pupil midwives to be there when the call came and to rush along the corridor, don a pair of rubber gloves, sprint to the couch and supervise (I use the word in jest) the delivery of the head — the rest usually followed without trouble.

Waiting, a large part of the business, was carried on ("suffered" might be a better word) in a small ante-room a few yards along the corridor from the Labour Ward. Its one concession to comfort was an ancient armchair, although any comfort gained in sitting in it was soon regretted when the occupant found that it was almost literally stuffed with fleas, countless generations of whose corpses lent a certain solidity to the cushions. This might have been tolerable, were it not that their descendants, all alive and very active, explored every occupant with a degree of promptness and enthusiasm that quickly turned what would have been the favourite chair into one which was all too readily offered to visitors. Investing in a pound of DDT powder which was heaved into the underside and back of the upholstery had but little effect, although we reckoned it slowed down their reproductive rate a bit. One or two of our number, more sensitive creatures than the rest of us, developed wheals halfway up their limbs and avoided that part of the room altogether, perching on bare wooden chairs in the corner while waiting for what was to them the relief of a call to the Labour Ward.

The other problem was the rubber gloves. Economy being the constant watchword, rubber gloves were not treated as disposable but were washed after use then rolled up in pairs and stored steeping in a bath of Dettol ready for the next hapless user to fish out and try to put on, often over massively flea-bitten hands and wrists. If you've never tried putting on a pair of soaking wet surgical gloves, take my tip — don't bother. Doing this almost led to trouble once: an urgent call down the corridor had me running into the Labour Ward heading as usual for the glove bucket, when Sister called out, "Hurry up, will you — she's nearly there!" Sister's voice was one of those voices that are not to be disobeyed — even a silent glare turned the legs to jelly for many a poor worm of a student, but it did nothing to speed up the struggle with the gloves. Time was running out

"Don't push! . . . Do-o-o-o-a-n't push, Missus!" she cried, in direct contradiction to her encouraging shouts of a few seconds earlier. By then, of course, the decision to push or not was out of the control of either party: in desperation, as I frantically flapped my fingers, she pushed the emerging head back in between heaves, the scalp becoming a bit more visible each time. "JUST COME ON!" she bawled, so I came, without more ado. She took away her restraining hand, the mother gave another push and the child was delivered. Well, sort of. Its head had had ample rehearsal of the process in the preceding minutes and its passage to the outside world was at express speed; I wasn't just ready and lunged for it; the wet, blue body met my hands, each finger dangling three inches of wet Dettol-soaked rubber, at about mother's knee level, where I caught it like a rugby ball — at least as well as you can catch a rugby ball with all those bits of rubber waving about.

"There now, Missus — you've a fine [a quick glance down] son!" The voice was kindly and sharing in the triumph; the look was at me and conveyed something quite different. I slunk off and began the post-procedure tidying-up. At least the head's repeated attempts to make its exit had caused enough stretching to avoid a maternal tear despite the high speed, showing that every cloud has a silver lining — if you look hard enough. My main thought at that stage was, "Thank God there's only one more to go!" Obstetrics was definitely not my thing — a physician I worked for years later shared my view succinctly: "Between the navel and the knees I only know women socially."

16

Fair Enough.

I do sometimes wonder about the baby, though; if, in later life, he displayed any strange attitudes to wet rubber . . . I would know why.

Once I and my cronies had got our quotas, we had a bit more time to enjoy the city and its surroundings, the time then passing much more quickly than it did in the acquisition of knowledge. Chris and I left a day early to detour up through the Midlands and Donegal — which is where we came in and why I came to be here.

CHAPTER
TWO

First Impressions

"Oh, yes, you'll be in Rathmore — I'll just get Miss Anderson, she has the keys." The young woman at the reception desk had a smiling welcome for us. We needed it, after a night on train and ferry, then hauling our worldly possessions behind us to find a car-hire place. An hour or two into an ever-bleaker countryside made more so by a dark wet winter's day made us wonder if this whole adventure hadn't been an awful mistake. My poor wife, who'd never set foot in the country before, was wondering what on earth I had seen in the place to wax so enthusiastic about it that she'd agreed to up sticks from the cosiness of Middle England to see the wonders of Ireland, while for me Winston Churchill's phrase referring to "the dreary steeples of Fermanagh and Tyrone" was beginning to sound dreadfully accurate as the countryside sloshed by.

I knew nothing of the place we were heading for — I hadn't even applied there and the letter offering a post came as a sort of *deus ex machina* just when all our applications had come to nothing. We accepted, wondering all the while how they knew about us — but then, this was Ireland.

A white-coated figure stopped by the desk. "You're starting here tomorrow, then?" (My, how word gets around — we'd only been there two minutes!) "You're taking my job, you see — I'm moving on."

"Ah," seemed the only reply I could muster.

"Going to Obs and Gynae, y'see — finished the general jobs."

The thought: "Well, Good Luck to you" crossed my mind as visions of Dublin surfaced again, but I just smiled; at least by now he'd have some idea of what was in store.

"Tell you what — I'm on tonight; when you get yourselves sorted out, come over about nine, 'cos I'll be doing a sedation round sometime then and I'll show you around the place."

"Thanks, I will."

So, while Alice set about turning the flat into as near a home as one could get with the contents of a couple of cases and a small trunk, I wandered over at the appointed time. The hospital was on the edge of the town and beyond the light of its windows rural blackness reigned. Even the town seemed just a group of lights in the darkness — no all-illuminating sodium glare here then.

I was within twenty yards or so of the main entrance when suddenly the door was flung open and a figure shot out of it — rather awkwardly, because my host for the evening had one hand on his collar and the other on his trouser backside. A good shove sent him reeling down the steps, where he lost his balance and fell, rolling to a stop on the ground before trying to pick himself up.

". . . and if you show your face in here again tonight — I'LL BREAK YOUR BLOODY NECK!" came from mine host, as his victim, now more or less on his feet and obviously very, very drunk, lurched off into the night, hurling imprecations which grew fainter as he disappeared from view into the blackness.

My new colleague spotted me (I'd come to a standstill, jaw-dropped-fascinated, during all this). "Come on in, you're just in time."

If this was part of the sedation round then it showed a remarkably original approach to therapy, but I wasn't entirely sure how to open a conversation about it. A raised eyebrow, a questioning look and a jab of a thumb in the direction of the fast-fading shouts had the desired effect: "One of our regulars — he's a real bastard when he's drunk — there's f — all else wrong with him, but he's been in and out all evening. Giving lip to me is one thing, but when he starts pushing the girls about, you don't put up with that!"

No, indeed.

How refreshing — none of this latter-day "referred for counselling and recognition of his addictive state", just an uncompromising "Get Out!"

The job description, almost non-existent by today's standards, hadn't said anything about being a bouncer, even part-time — maybe it was taken for granted out here and not thought worthy of separate mention. I flexed my biceps and joined in the sedation round.

It may come as a disappointment to learn that over the next four decades I never found reason or opportunity to do the same — probably just as well, really: you could get struck off for that sort of thing these days — but the guy probably deserved it and it worked; he didn't come back again that night, anyway.

After such an introduction, the realities of the job over the following months and years turned out to be remarkably orthodox — hard work, long hours, making decisions you felt not quite qualified enough to make with confidence — in short, being thrown in at the Deep End. Help was on hand if you really did need it and was given so willingly that you made it a point of honour not to call unless the need was unequivocal. It was a very happy ship.

These days, if you want a career in Medicine, you need to have its course plotted out while you're still a foetus, right down to the obligatory research project. Drifting around just isn't on, while drifting into a job is anathema to the Organisation. But life was freer and easier then, and all the better for it — you could sample something and either stick with it or move on, depending on how you took to it. Alice and I both sampled aspects of that Broad Church that is Medicine and then fell, almost accidentally, into bits that suited us down to the ground.

It nearly went wrong, however.

One morning the phone rang in my office; it was J, one of our GP colleagues who'd been in his practice since the Flood — or at least for the better part of half a century.

"Tell me — would you ever fancy joining me in the practice?" The invitation came almost out of the blue, although we'd struck up a (largely telephonic) friendship over the few years I'd been there.

"Err — I don't know," was all I could say. "Let me think about it for a few days and I'll come back to you."

Eventually, reluctant to burn any boats, especially the rather comfortable one I'd settled in, I reckoned I could try a three-week stint, exchanging holiday time for a sample of full-time General Practice.

This wouldn't be quite my first experience of the work, although previous toe-dipping had been confined to very short-term cover for some of the locals in exchange for a crisp fiver a night — a fortune then. My first ever call in this capacity showed me how different General Practice was from what until then I'd thought was "Real Medicine" — in fact it is the General Practice that is real, the rest of us often living in white-coated isolation from many of the facts of medical life.

"Is it you that's covering for Dr McLean?" came the voice bellowing into the other end of the phone — clearly a man not prepared to trust his communication to electricity.

"Yes." I held the phone further away.

"Well you'd need to come and see the missus — she's wild bad the night."

"What's wrong with her?"

"Ach, now she's wild bad: ye'd need til come out til her."

This was getting nowhere, so capitulation seemed the only option.

"OK; where do you live?"

"Just out the road a bit."

"Which road?"

"Dae ye know Willy Joe McCracken's house?"

"No, I don't, not at all."

"Well, our lane's just a whean o' yards afore ye get til him, now."

It took some time to worm out from him even an approximate idea of where he lived, by which time it was plain that we each considered the other an idiot, although at least my opinion was a professional one.

"Sure, I'll leave a milk can at the lane end: that way you'll not miss it."

Great — a landmark!

Probably it wasn't entirely his fault that every laneway in the county had a creamery can at its end that night, presumably awaiting collection in the morning, but my patience, already stretched, was at twanging point by the time I finally got to his door, directed with the help of his more cerebrate neighbours, some of whom filled me in with details of my patient-to-be, things I'd never have thought of asking about. It seemed there was nothing secret in this community.

I saw her, treated her and left, all without gleaning the faintest idea of what was wrong with her. I was only a little reassured the following morning when I reported on my night's work to Dr Mac — "Sure, she's been to every doctor in the Six Counties and nobody knows what's ailing her. I reckon it's all in her head."

A useful, and remarkably common, diagnosis in General Practice.

Some months later I was offered a weekend of cover in another practice — a Friday night surgery, an "Urgents" surgery on Saturday morning and the rest of the time on call. Surgery was in the house and I had the place to myself.

"I've warned the regulars not to bother you, so things should be OK," said John, as he prepared to leave. "The only thing that's likely to have you out is Mrs O'Hare, out at Drumnahouge; she's due at any time — in fact, I thought she'd have delivered yesterday."

Thoughts of Dublin and domiciliary obstetrics must have affected my expression, for he went on: "Don't worry, I've left the Midder bag out with her and Mollie's looking after her." This news brought at least modified relief: Mollie was then in the prime of her career as District Midwife — five foot nothing, with eyes pointing in wildly different directions, she had a heart of gold and a tongue that could blister paint at fifty yards when she was riled. She drove an ancient Austin 8, whose continued mobility defied the efforts of time and its owner. She could see the road (with one or other eye) only through the spokes of the steering wheel and the bottom inch or two of windscreen: on the road the car gave the impression of being driven by a nurse's hat.

But she knew her patients and apparently was not averse to creaming off some of the more affluent layettes: "I know ones as couldn't even get a one o' them nice things and sure that wean doesn't need all that stuff now, does he?" Most mothers thus approached found that "No" wasn't an option in the reply, so Mollie acted as a redistributor of wealth in her patch — and to tell the truth was generally admired for it, even by the donors.

She had a deep knowledge of her clientele, both mothers and offspring, and followed them long after her formal commitments to them were over. While it must be said that her practice was totally ethical and even-handed, Mollie was of solid Republican stock, with an attitude to the Royal Ulster Constabulary that was in keeping with it. Legend has it that once, while driving, she was stopped by an officious young RUC constable out to impress his accompanying Sergeant, to remonstrate with her over some minor traffic infringement. His lecture was interrupted: "Would your name be —?" said Mollie, eyeing him as only she could.

"Er — well — er — yes," said the young man, quite taken aback.

"Jesus, Mary and Joseph! I thought it was you — last time I saw you I was smacking your backside to start you breathing — and this is how you end up, is it?"

There's not a lot you can say to that, especially when her other eye appeared to be exchanging the merest hint of a wink with the accompanying Sergeant — who had just developed an awkward facial twitch. The poor lad just stood open-mouthed as Mollie found a gear and let in the clutch.

I reckon the Sergeant put him up to it.

So at least one of us would have some experience, even if it wasn't me.

Sure as Fate, John had hardly been gone an hour when the call came. I got directions: the place was an isolated cottage, a long way into the foothills of the mountains. The midwife had already been called (maybe they'd heard about me and got their priorities right), so I set off thinking, "If I go slowly maybe it'll all be over by the time I get there," rehearsing the while the manoeuvres for atypical presentations, as far as could remember them.

In the event, however, this time I did quite genuinely lose my way and only after a couple of enquiries of folks living at the ends of long lanes (everybody there seemed to live at the end of a long lane) did I finally see the Austin parked on the verge outside the cottage.

"Great!" I thought. "She's here first."

I knocked and went into the little hallway.

"She's in there, Doctor." The husband was playing his husbandly role and confining himself to the kitchen.

I pushed open the bedroom door.

An overpowering stench of chloroform hit me, probably accentuated by the heat in the room from an open fire blazing halfway up the chimney. Two or three breaths of this and I was already feeling a bit light-headed; I thanked God, and John, that it was the non-flammable chloroform and not the explosive ether: had it been ether I reckoned the roof would have been off now and my problems would not have been Obstetric, but Forensic.

The baby was delivered, washed, cuddled up and quiet in mother's arms; I'd even missed the delivery of the placenta. Mollie was at the head of the bed, the Midder bag open beside her, wielding the gauze mask and a large dropper bottle of chloroform, most of whose contents were already in the atmosphere.

"I don't hold with this newfangled stuff, but I thought I'd better give her a bit seeing as how you were so . . . delayed."

(Newfangled! It's been around since 1840, for God's sake! Even Mollie wasn't that old.)

Having confirmed the absence of any perineal tear, checked pulse and blood pressure and assured myself that the baby had no obvious problems, I felt that I had become redundant. Mollie said nothing, but I think she shared that view.

Mother and Father thanked me effusively as I left; Mollie was silent, but shifted one of her gazes to me and let the shadow of a grin cross her face.

She knew.

I learned very quickly that rural General Practice is the real sharp end of Medicine and not for the faint-hearted, even when you've managed to find your way to where you're needed in the pitch dark with the rain coming down faster than the wipers can cope with it.

One such night I was summoned almost to the furthest end of John's patch — and John's patch was a big one: it contained his share of the town's population but went out far into the peat bogs and hills; a countryside of stunted trees, scrub, sedge, little fields of poor pasture and a scattering of farmsteads, all without electricity, mains water or drainage.

A slow sloshing drive got me to a house visible only by the glimmer of an oil lamp in the window. The headlights picked out a cart parked on its end in the rough stone-and-moss-floored yard, while above the whitewashed walls there seemed to be a roof of mouldering thatch. The place looked much as it must have done two centuries and more ago.

The door was opened to me: "Sorry to bring you out so far on such a night, Doctor — she's upstairs, this way." Any annoyance at being called out evaporates when the opening greeting is, "Sorry" — and they're usually the ones who have genuine need of an out-of-hours visit.

The walls of the only downstairs living room, dimly lit by an oil lamp hanging from a ceiling beam, seemed wholly in keeping with the age-old appearance of the outside; only a couple of mouldy-edged photographs on the walls told you this was the twentieth century, not the eighteenth. The whitewashed walls and the thatch might have made it picturesque on a good day, but the realities of living under a leaking roof they couldn't afford to fix, on an earth floor which turned to mud if any of the outside wet got onto it, with an open hearth turf fire the sole source of heating, would soon dispel any illusions of The Good Life.

The bedroom, as was often the case in these houses, comprised an upper floor open like a gallery and occupying about three-quarters of the area of the room below. At least this one had a fixed stair: there were still some that had only a ladder for access by the agile, while subdivision into bedrooms was unknown, any privacy coming from a bit of curtain. We made our way to one side of this, where the roof dropped down almost to floor level, leaving only a foot or so of wall height to accommodate a tiny window. The bed was hard up against the wall, making half of it almost uninhabitable for want of headroom: it was covered in a mass of home-made quilts and grey ex-army blankets. A hump under this mound, well into the distant uninhabitable bit, identified my patient.

"Can you bring the lamp over a wee bit?" I asked, for its bearer had held back, presumably diffident at encroaching on a consultation, even with a relative. The story was one of acute abdominal pain and even with the oil lamp held as close as possible a full clinical examination was just not feasible: in addition to the pile of quilts and blankets, she was clad in innumerable layers of clothing, ensuring her skin was well separated from the outside world. I began, as delicately as one can in such circumstances, to feel her abdomen, having to climb onto the bed to do so, keeping low enough to avoid the rafters and the twig-and-straw mix that hung down between them and separated us (more or less) from the pouring rain above. Any stranger happening

29

upon the sight could have been forgiven for seeing it as some bizarre and awkward, indeed perverse, sexual assault, even more so as a great deal of groping was needed just to find the belly: once it had been found and a few anatomical landmarks identified, it became, relatively speaking, plain sailing.

This looked like gall-bladder disease, most likely a stone on the move giving rise to the pain. The idea of looking for jaundice was laughable: in the flickering flame of the hurricane lamp we all looked yellow. Like so many diagnoses, this was a Best Guess job and this was the best guess. I sorted out the then-standard treatment: "That should settle things in half an hour or so, I think — do give me a shout again if she doesn't improve."

"Ach, now, Doctor, we wouldn't want to bring you out all this way again — I'm sure she'll be just fine."

They were the sort of people I'd willingly have gone out again for; hospitable, polite, charming, respectful without any feeling of subservience, they and their likes (and there are still many of them), the unassuming salt of the Earth, make the job worthwhile.

It's one thing to do the occasional one-night stand but quite another to take up full-time practice: I wasn't at all sure that I was cut out for it and the three-week stint, carrying my full share of the job, convinced me that my temperament wasn't of the sort that would stand up to this for a lifetime. Almost my first call-out made that clear, when a middle-aged man "came over weak" in the council office next door to the surgery, a few steps away from us. So what did he do? He walked the two miles home and rang for the doctor to come out as an emergency! A newcomer to the area, I got lost in the countryside, panic rising in me. Finally I found the house, after a couple of tries at wrong addresses, and rang the door bell. It was answered promptly by a lady in her sixties, whose puzzled look at first made me feel that I'd found yet another wrong address.

"I'm sorry, but I'm looking for a Robert . . ."

"Oh, yes he's here, but he's not ill, Doctor." (I didn't know them, but they knew me — even by then, I suspect that most of the practice knew "the new man".)

She looked back into the house. Robert was sitting in his chair by the fire, plainly physically comfortable, but he was beginning to squirm under the eye of his mother.

"Aye, it's — er — it's me, Doctor. I took a bit of a weak turn in the council offices and I thought I'd better — get — it — checked — out." His voice trailed off, his mother and I staring at him in disbelief.

"You were in the Council Offices?" I asked him, astounded. "Why didn't you call in on us, for heaven's sake? We're only next door!"

Mother was even more forthright: "What on earth are you thinking of?" The word "fool" formed silently on her lips, but saw no audible expression — at least while I was there.

There was of course nothing wrong with him that a sound telling-off wouldn't cure, but I felt I could safely leave that to his mother, who looked well set for battle as she showed me to the door, apologising for her son's behaviour all the way. I got the impression that she'd been trying to get him off her hands, married and responsible for himself, for years, so far to no avail.

I never saw him again professionally, though he did once cross the street to avoid me.

Three weeks of this and I had acquired migraine, insomnia and dyspepsia all in fair measure and had become, I was told, even more unliveable-with than usual. I fled back to my niche and declined the offer with thanks ". . . but, we've been talking it over and if you're interested Alice might be keen enough to take it on."

"Would she now?" came the reply. "Well, if she'd be interested I'd be very happy to have her — get her to come round tonight and we'll talk it over."

With those few exchanges the course of our lives was set: Alice would do the Practice, I would keep my day job and do the on-call out of hours. It was an arrangement that suited us both, for general practice was Alice's metier, while I kept a foot in both camps to be part of that world of tragedy, pathos and downright farce (sometimes all at the same time) that is Medicine.

CHAPTER
THREE

New Brooms

So there we were, General Practitioners, though not so much fully-fledged as still-naked nestlings. However, like all of us at that stage of life and work, we were determined to set new, ever-higher standards of Scientific Medicine in the town and to banish the mumbo-jumbo of our predecessors: not for us the actions of our immediate predecessor, who coped with his difficult cases by ensuring that the blame for failure was placed squarely where it belonged — on the patient.

The arrival on the market of the two-colour capsule gave him an unprecedented opportunity to pursue this policy:

"Doctor, them new capsule things ye gave me's no good — I'm not one bit better than I was when I started them."

"Tell me, how did you take them?"

"Ach, just with a wee taste o' water to get them down, Doctor."

"Yes, of course, but which end did you swallow first?"

"Ach, God, Doctor, I wouldn't know — didn't take any notice o' that, now."

"Well, now, there's your answer — you need to swallow them red end first — if you take them upside down they'll never do you a bit of good."

"Oh . . . er . . . right, Doctor — I didn't know."

"Never mind, I'll give you another week's worth — now mind you get them down the right way."

"Yes, Doctor."

And off he went, with an activity to keep him occupied (pretty fully too, I imagine) until Mother Nature sorted him out in her own time.

Diagnostic mysteries were never admitted to:

"Doctor, I've an awfu' sore knee."

The offending part is examined, then, very seriously:

"Charlie, did ever you have anything like this before?"

"No, Doctor."

(Pause)

"Well, you've got it now!"

"Oh, God save us, Doctor!"

Who needs a name for a disease?

There was to be none of this for us and there would be no nonsense about inappropriate out-of-hours calls. Our attempts at discipline in the practice eventually brought about a sea change in our own attitudes as we came to realise that the great bulk of out-of-hours calls were by our standards "inappropriate" and could have been left until the next day without any harm accruing.

Gross abuse we would not tolerate in the way our predecessors had done and from the first we adopted the "Admiral Byng" principle — shoot one (or in our case half a dozen) to encourage the others: those who blatantly abused the service were given their marching orders, along with those very few who were rude or aggressive to staff. In a community like this, word of these hitherto-unknown sanctions spread like wildfire: "Ye'd best not be crossing them or they'll be putting you off — then where'd ye go?"

The counterpart of this, of course, is to do your damnedest for those who really need you. Some of this seemed to be filtering through at a fairly early stage, when I was called to a house halfway up the hillside one night to see a sick child. As I was leaving, standing in the steady rain on the farmhouse step, repeating my advice to make sure it got home, a figure lurched into the faint pool of light cast by the bulb over the door.

"Oh, hello, Pat," said the mother of the house. "Come on in — it's no night to be outside."

The figure approached and rolled up towards me — there were no prizes for guessing where he'd spent the last few hours, even without smelling his breath — small, wiry, of indeterminate age but probably well over the hump of middle life. A mackintosh with the collar turned up blended with a cap pulled well down over his forehead and hiding the upper part of his face. Small and spare, he had the air of a superannuated whippet; all he needed to complete the caricature was a squint, but his eyes were hidden in the shadow of his cap.

"This is the new doctor, Pat, Dr Alport. He's just been in to see wee Angela."

He cocked his head to one side and scanned me up and down. I still couldn't see his eyes.

"Doctor Alfred, is it?" he cackled (it took ages for some of them to get the name right, although the same ones could tackle unhesitatingly a long Irish polysyllabic with hordes of redundant consonants that would leave an Englishman dumbstruck). "Ach now, I've hear'd tell o' you — round here they're saying, 'If Dr Alfred says ye're done — *ye're done!*'" With that he cackled again, came up the steps and headed indoors.

I said goodnight and got into the car. I felt I'd been paid a compliment, although that might just have been his way of being polite to a newcomer.

Even by then, the value of "Scientific Medicine" was beginning to assume its true level and we accepted that what was important wasn't the depth of knowledge of Physiology, Pathology or Biochemistry, but how you presented yourself as a caring practitioner — something that goes beyond the oft-derided "bedside manner" and is a reflection of what you are and what you hope the community will think of you. Be sure they'll soon have you sussed out and pretty well summed up anyway, so make sure they've got the best impression you can give them!

Get things right and no one says anything, but get one or two things unequivocally wrong and it takes years to repair the damage to a hard-earned reputation. Sometimes the best tack is to use that sadly all-too-rare approach, the apology.

Irene was one of our "regulars" — a frequent attender with a different set of symptoms each time: as middle age gained its grip on her she became steadily more overweight, with all the aches and pains that came from carrying around a few extra stones. Inevitably this came to include backache. Then one day — an urgent house call in mid-afternoon: the backache was much, much worse. Now, give Irene her due, when she made contact, it was always at the surgery and this was a departure from the norm: it should have rung alarm bells, but it didn't; call it lack of experience or whatever.

The visit revealed nothing except some ill-localised tenderness around her lower back and I began my descent into ignominy by launching into a long stern lecture on the perils and problems of being overweight. (Well, it made me feel superior, slim healthy-looking creature that I was then.) I left her with a prescription for pain relief and a load of guilt and misery, mainly of my own making.

A further call a couple of days later ran pretty much the same course: still the alarm bells were silent.

It was almost a week later that I saw her name in the appointments list for the morning clinic. "Ah, obviously my choice of pain killer has been a brilliant one and has got her back on her feet in no time at all," thought I. (Even now, writing this decades later, I marvel at my own arrogance and stupidity.)

She came in, looking well, happy and noticeably slimmer. "She's obviously taken my dieting advice to heart," was the first thought — the arrogant self-satisfaction was getting into top gear.

She sat down and beamed at me: "I thought maybe you should see this, Doctor." She handed over a small, clear specimen bottle: as I looked at its contents the penny dropped — and the sound was deafening. Inside the bottle lay the largest kidney stone I had ever seen and I thought I saw just the faintest flicker of superiority in the smile ("I told you I was sick . . .").

There was a silence as she looked at me, smiling.

I took a deep breath: "Irene, I think I owe you a very deep apology; I'm afraid I got this completely wrong and I will understand if you'd rather transfer to another practice."

She looked almost shocked: "Ach now, Doctor, dear me; there's none of us perfect, sure: them as never made a mistake never made anything, y'know. I'd not dream of going anywhere else." Magnanimity in victory indeed.

By the time the (necessarily lengthened) consultation was over, we were much closer than we'd ever been and laughing together. "Well," I said as she went to leave, "you've fairly taught me a few lessons this morning, I can tell you." Her laugh in reply contained no iota of superiority.

Investigations, which I pushed on as urgently as I could (I felt I owed at least that to her), revealed a serious underlying problem which made her a familiar figure at local and regional hospital specialist units, as well as a very frequent visitor to the surgery. Treatment did, however, clear up most of her odd and previously undiagnosable symptoms and she has remained well: although we've helped to see her through some of the tragedies of life since then and seen her at her lowest, we've always had a warm smile for each other, an unspoken reminiscence. Yes, if one had a pecking order of patients, Irene'd be high on it.

CHAPTER FOUR

Settling In

It's a sign that you're settling in when you start to get visits to the Regulars — those who've been seen at home for more years than they or their attendants can remember and who can't cope with the idea of seeing anyone other than "their" doctor, although they would make an allowance for holidays, protracted sickness — or death.

One such was Sally.

Sally lived out in the country on her own, in a big dilapidated old house that had once, maybe a century ago, been the centre of a reasonably prosperous farm, but which was now little more than a yard overgrown to the point where you could hardly see where it began and ended, with a ramshackle collection of collapsing outhouses now used as a hay store by the neighbouring farmer who had bought up the land as the estate fell on progressively harder times and was gradually broken up.

Sally didn't get out much — in fact, she didn't get out at all. To say she had varicose ulcers was to extend the definition of the condition — her legs were virtually completely circumferentially ulcerated between knees and ankles, festering gently as they had done for decades. J called regularly, having her in his little book of "Those To Be Seen Weekly". Despite him and the District Nurse, years of treatment had seen little change, though at least so far there was no sign of any malignant transformation at the edges. She was adamant in her refusal to have anything more than dressing done for them and spent her days in an armchair with her legs up on a stool, the home help and the neighbours keeping her going from week to week.

She'd been one of J's "specials" and I'd been around for some time before I was asked to see her. I knew the medical background, but was soon to wish I'd been told more.

I found the back door open and knocked — no reply. A shout of, "Hello, it's the doctor" brought a muffled response from the depths: "Just come you in, Doctor." So in I went, into a hallway gloomy beyond belief, even on this bright spring day. Following the source of the voice took me down corridors which seemed extraordinarily narrow for the size of the place; it was only as my eyes adapted to the gloom that I saw that the walls were lined, floor to ceiling, with cardboard boxes — butter boxes, washing-powder boxes, grocery boxes of all descriptions, most of them seemingly packed with newspapers, or at least those newspapers that didn't litter the floor. There was also the oddest of smells — dust, dirt, old musty paper, a vague smell of what might be sepsis, old food and a strange smell like neglected armpits, but not quite identifiable. Some of the lower boxes smelt of urine, having presumably soaked it up from the floor: what had put it there in the first place was not apparent and frankly it wasn't my business to find out here and now. People live in funny ways and short of hoisting them out and incarcerating them in a nice clean tidy prison of a ward or nursing home (which destroys them but makes us feel better), you simply take them as they are — they're used to it and comfortable in their own way.

Sally was in the armchair, feet up as usual: she could have done with being about five stones lighter, but had a cheery smile for me, a stranger to her.

"Me legs are getting awful sore, Doctor; they didn't get dressed this week — I wonder would you ever look at them?"

I squatted down facing her, my bag on the floor beside her: floor space was limited, for the boxes, hundreds of them, filled what was really quite a big room and left only mini-corridors between the stacks, around which her visitors navigated — a sort of cardboard Hampton Court Maze. I wondered idly if anyone had wandered off among the boxes and never come back — God, maybe THAT was the smell!

I'd just finished cleaning the first leg when there was a soft, slightly snuffly intake of air behind me, then a waft of hot smelly breath drifted down around the back of my neck, seeming to go on for ages. I knew there was no one else in the house and the experience, as I waited, frozen, for the strangler's grip, was not so much heart-stopping, more knicker-wetting, as the terror rose in me and the adrenaline surged.

"Ach, now," said Sally, who, facing me and whatever was behind me, hadn't batted an eyelid, "he'll do ye no harm — he's just curious."

Very little reassured I turned — and met the nostrils, lips and solemn gaze of a large chestnut horse.

A HORSE! Here in the living room!

It was some time before I regained my balance, physical and psychological; however, a life in general practice teaches you never to be surprised (well, not *too* surprised) at anything. I swallowed hard and smiled at him. By way of reply he showed me his teeth; not in any malevolent way but just as a friendly greeting, giving me in the process a waft of his halitosis that I could have done without.

I was still holding the roll of bandage I'd been about to apply before perceptions of the world shifted, its free end dangling unhygenically close to the floor. Gathering my wits and trying to look as if this happened in every house I visited, I began bandaging. He looked on almost over my shoulder, concerned and studious, like a clinical tutor checking on a student's practical skills. (Come to think of it, he'd probably seen it done often enough to have an opinion on it.)

Sally fished around her seat and found an apple that had been wedged down somewhere in the recesses of the chair: "Here, give him this — he's looking an apple at this time o' day." Too fazed to suggest other things she could do with it, I handed it to the horse. He took it politely and cleanly, munching on it. Then he farted and I discovered the mystery ingredient in the cocktail of smells . . .

"Oh, didn't you know about the horse? I thought everyone knew about him," said the receptionist when I returned, full of the experience. I might have believed her if she hadn't been grinning quite so mischievously.

"No, I damn well didn't and it's only by the grace of God that I don't need a change of underwear. At least I'll know for next time. Er — she doesn't keep anything else, now — does she?"

Inevitably in so uncompromisingly rural an area, human medicine brings you close to the lives of the animals that make up so much of the scenery here; sheep on the upper slopes, hardy black cattle on the rough upland pastures and fat dairy herds on the bits of better ground lower down. Pig rearing shares the lowland terrain when there's any money to be made, the economics of it determining just how much there is of it at any one time.

It was a night of a hard frost and I was glad enough that this call was not too far away; even so, it was far enough off the beaten track to make it seem well away from civilisation, the steading snuggled at the bottom of a hill down a long lane and almost hidden in the trees until you were nearly on top of it. A solitary bulb burned in the window, the grubby curtains pulled back to let some of the light fall onto the yard so that I could find the door.

Inside, the place was minimalist — a black range, only just alight; a couple of chairs, neither entirely intact, set against a table that looked as if it had not been cleared, let alone cleaned and set, for years. That and a sofa whose stuffing was winning the battle against its confinement constituted the contents of the room. In short, just the sort of place I'd grown to expect of a bachelor household. Two brothers, both now in their seventies, had drifted along in the old house for all their lives, seeking neither spouses nor housekeepers, but simply doing what was necessary when it became necessary or, rather, when it became impossible to manage with it as it was.

Their attitude to the practice was in keeping and we rarely heard from them, so when you were called at night you didn't argue; something was really wrong.

"It's Charlie, Doctor: he's had the 'flu this past day or two, but he's real bad tonight, so he is." Will looked worried, his grimy face drawn and haggard. It was more than just the natural concern for an ailing brother — the two of them needed to be fit in order to keep the farm afloat, a task that was getting no easier as the years went by. What would happen if one of them wasn't there was something that they'd probably never discussed aloud, but it must have loomed over them like a black cloud before the eventual deluge.

He led me into the other room of the house, a bedroom sparsely enough furnished; a bed, a couple of chairs, a dilapidated wardrobe and what had once been a nice enough dressing table, all set on a threadbare carpet, made up the total of the fixed contents. The room was bitterly cold — there was no heating and the fire looked as if it had not been lit in decades. The water streamed down the walls, mainly from condensation of vapour: the source of some of the vapour lay in

45

the bed. It was the classical Bed-End diagnosis — toxic and ill, his breathing shallow and — the clincher — gross sores of herpes simplex all around his lips and nose. Here was a typical pneumococcal pneumonia; all I needed to complete the diagnosis was to listen to his chest to find out the side affected. That was easy; it was the next bit that became unexpectedly difficult.

"He really needs to be in hospital tonight . . ."

"I'm going to no hospital — not tonight, not any night." These were almost the first words Charlie had uttered and the effort was hurting him. Persuasion, remonstration, cajoling, all were in vain. I'd been around long enough to know when to give up, so settled for a massive shot of penicillin.

"Can we get a bit of heat into this place?" I asked. "It's freezing in here. Can we light a fire or something? He needs a bit of warmth."

"Sure, that fire's all blocked up: there hasn't been a fire lit in there this many a long year," said Will.

"Well, do you have an electric fire or something?"

"Ah, now — never had one o' them things." Then an idea came to him — you could tell by the light that came into his face and spread over into a smile of triumph in discovery.

"I could mebbie get one of the heat lamps from out the pig house; would that help, d'ye think?"

We headed out across the sparkling frost of the yard and into the pigs' accommodation, a large wooden building. It seemed to be in darkness, but as he opened the door a flood of light poured out. He stood aside to let me go in first, but what I saw stopped me in my tracks and he had to nudge me aside to close the door behind me. By the standards of the place we'd just left it was the ultimate in luxury: well-lit, comfortably draught-free and gloriously warm from rows of heat lamps beaming down on lots of sows with their piglets, most of them fast asleep on thick beds of clean straw. It occurred to me to suggest that the best answer to the problem might be for Charlie to move in here and, just for once, let the pigs suffer the conditions their owners were putting up with — I still rather regret that I said nothing about it.

A lamp was quickly detached and taken into the bedroom to replace the miserable bulb above the bed. This was about as much as we were going to do tonight, so I soon headed home.

After all, there's money in pigs and you can't afford to lose one . . . even if it kills you.

Old pig farmers are harder to kill than that, however. I went back next morning to find Charlie sitting up in bed and looking and sounding a great deal brighter.

"Sure, I knew there was no need to be traipsing off to the hospital — I'm rightly now — be on my feet in a whean o' days, so I will."

And indeed he was, back into the back-breaking round of toil with no end, just to keep going until the Deluge, in whatever final form, would descend on one, and thus on both, of them. Until then . . . you just keep going.

★   ★   ★

Maybe there's something about pigs that inspires a rather closer relationship than you usually find with other farm animals; they're intelligent and may well enjoy human company, though it's best not to think of this when you're biting into your ham sandwich or tackling your second rasher of a morning. It salves the conscience a bit when the pig comes off best.

It was an afternoon in late spring and just for once the place was quiet, the locals all seeming to have found other things to do than to come and bother us. The paperwork was all up to date (any doctor reading this will realise that this was a long time ago) and a cup of tea seemed in order. Sod's Law being what it is, of course, the kettle had just come to the boil when a noise in the waiting room — a thumping, dragging sound punctuated by yelps and groans — told us that tea was going onto the Long Finger.

"Hell — wouldn't you know, just when you think you'd get a wee cup in peace," came from Staff Nurse as she put down the teapot and followed me to the door (well, I was nearest to it).

Two men were crossing the room towards us, each supporting the other and providing the groans and yelps in fair measure as they did. With the help of staff and a wheelchair we got them onto trolleys and enquired the cause of this odd affair.

"Well, you see, we were killing a pig — and he got away."

"So how come you end up like this?"

It seemed that the pair had decided to shoot the pig and after a chase had caught it: one of the pair had taken the creature by its ears, straddling its neck and steadying it, while the other, standing with his back to a low parapet wall, had brought the gun (a .22 rifle — not the most appropriate tool for the job) to the pig's forehead.

As I've said, pigs are not stupid and even the dimmest of the race would have realised that all was not sweetness and light here. This pig was no exception and chose his response perfectly, lunging forward just as the trigger was pulled. The gunman was head-butted hard enough to push him over the parapet, while the shot went into the right foot of the captor, who by then was on the ground anyway, Piggy's lunge having left him unsupported.

So with one badly bruised back, one bullet wound to foot and a pig last seen bolting for the horizon, we reckoned that was Game, Set and Match: whatever they did to it in the end, it looked like it was going to have a fairly lengthy stay of execution — no one was going to be fit to touch it for weeks.

No, pigs are not at all stupid.

Pigs may not be stupid, but their young can be delicate: like us they have no thick coat of fur, but unlike us, they don't have the clothing to compensate for that. Pig lamps are all very well, but do cost a bit to install and run.

A call came in at the end of afternoon surgery, sent in as non-urgent. "Just when you've a minute, Doctor

— could you call on Annie Parker, for she's not too well?"

I knew Annie; by then she was about eighty and still independent, playing a full part in running the small establishment they called a farm, although in Scotland it would have been described as a croft — a little thatched cottage, a couple of thatched outhouses and a very few acres of very middling pasture. I saw her occasionally, but she was an independent soul and looked after herself most of the time, so I reckoned that a detour on my way home would be better than leaving it until tomorrow.

It was an evening in late January, the sun newly set and its light still in the clear sky, portending a frosty night as a crescent moon showed itself over the hills to the east. I turned into the lane, a typical rough track better fitted to a tractor (these days, a four-wheel-drive saloon would cope perfectly with it — but they were far in the future then, if you disregard the go-anywhere Land Rover).

The house was as it always was and very likely always had been for a couple of centuries or more (although it had been better maintained than many of its contemporaries, most of them relegated to the status of ruinous outhouses). It had kept all its traditional features, not from sentiment or an antiquarian desire to retain originality, but simply because it worked well enough for their needs. The floor was of the usual beaten earth, while heat, cooking and a good deal of the lighting came from an open-hearth turf fire, which was glowing brightly, the light throwing long shadows all around the room, shadows which, while they didn't actually dance, were made living by the flickering turf flames. It was nice to feel the radiant heat as I came in the door (these houses had no porch, the outer door opening straight into the living room). Not all the radiant heat was coming my way, however: a part of its was blocked by a large tea chest on its side in front of the fire. Annie was in a chair beside the tea chest, while her son, a man in his late forties or early fifties by then, was kneeling at the other side of it, the pair of them seemingly basking before the fire's glow.

Annie's dress was as traditional as the house itself: an ankle-length black dress over which an almost equally large black shawl was thrown, the combination contriving to cover all of her save her ankles and a white circle of a face.

"Ach, hello, Doctor," she said, at the same time drawing out from the folds of the shawl a tiny pink object which uttered a short high-pitched cry as it met the outside world. A comment about baby-sitting stopped at the lips as I realised that this cute pink thing was in fact an almost new-born piglet. By now I'd moved far enough into the room to see over the tea chest and was rewarded by the sight of a whole litter of similar piglets stretched out in front of the hearth, some of them indeed edging towards the fire far enough to be into the hot ash at the foot of the burning turf. A comfortable snuffling and cheeping emanated from them — contentment indeed.

Annie's son explained that, while the whole family, Annie included, had been out "at the Moss", taking

51

advantage of an unusually dry spell of weather to start cutting turf for the fuel store, their sow had had her litter: the coldness of the day had already seen some of the piglets become a bit hypothermic, so all had been brought indoors.

As much to provide space for me to join the group in front of the tea chest as to keep discipline among his charges, he gathered up a bundle of them and put them unceremoniously back into the tea chest to a chorus of annoyance: young they may have been but they'd already acquired a taste for comfort and cosiness and the continued protests from the depths of the tea chest made it very likely that they'd be out again as soon as I'd stopped usurping their space.

This had hijacked my planned brief visit — after all, it's not something you can either ignore or not make the subject of some sort of conversation, however brief. Besides, there's something appealing about neonates of any species (perhaps it stirs the mothering instinct in us) and I was happy enough to chat for a while about the perils of pig-keeping before getting down to the purpose of the visit. I had already gathered that Annie wasn't really ill at all and all I could deduce from examining her was that she had no more than a mild upper respiratory infection. She didn't need a house call but I was glad I'd gone, just for the glimpse of an older Ireland that I'd been privileged to have (and one I had to suppress when defending the Irish against snooty English friends who thought they *all* kept pigs in the parlour!).

After my words of general advice, I left, pausing at the door to add, half over my shoulder, "Mind you don't snuggle up too close to them, now — you wouldn't want to be giving them your cold after all you've done for them, now, would you?"

CHAPTER
FIVE

The Bad,
the Mad and...

Life moves on and now that we were established in practice, it was our turn to be looking for locums on the odd night when we were on call and couldn't change with any of the partners. Just as we had done calls for our GP colleagues, now we were making the same offers to those of the hospital staff who were willing to exchange a night's work for a bunch of crisp notes. Usually help came from those who were intending to enter general practice — it perhaps gave them a sniff of it before they became irrevocably committed to the job, so different from the ordered life of the hospital. Len was one of our regulars, if two or three stints a year can be called regular.

"Would you fancy doing next Tuesday night for us, if you're free?" The usual request met with the usual response: "Yeah, sure — how long for and how much?"

I caught up with him on the Wednesday morning and the promised bunch of notes changed hands.

"How did it go — anything interesting?"

"That's the last bloody night I'll ever do on that f — ing practice — never again!"

"Uh? What was wrong?"

The concern was genuine — there weren't many of his calibre around and if he quit we could have trouble getting reliable cover at short notice.

He warmed to his story:

"I got this call out to Tirmallon, way up towards the end of the road. Got to the house, found the patient was the mother of this great big family and all of them in the room together. Anyway, it looked as if she had some sort of acute abdomen and I reckoned she needed to be down the road. I asked for the phone and one of the sons — at least that's who I took him to be — said: 'We've no phone here, but there's a phone box just a mile or so down the road. I'll go with you, for it's easy to miss.'

"So off we go and about three-quarters of a mile down the road this guy steps out into the road and waves us down. He's wearing a black balaclava and he's carrying a gun . . ."

"AK 47?" I interrupted, perhaps more flippantly than I should have done.

"I don't know and I don't f — ing care. When you're looking down the muzzle, the type is not that important — in fact, it's f — ing academic."

"Sorry, er — go on."

"Anyway, this guy stops us, pokes the gun through the window and says, 'Who are you and what do you want here?' I tell you, I was ready to shit myself, but then the bloke in the car, the son, leans over from the passenger side and says: 'This is the doctor — he's just been to see Mammy; she's sick and we're just going to phone for an ambulance, 'cos doctor says she might need an operation.'

"The guy drops the gun, leans in through the window and says: 'Jeez, I'm sorry to hear that — that's terr', if she's going to need an operation.' Then he looks at me and says, all very friendly-like, 'You go on, Doc — we'll see the ambulance gets through all right, don't you worry.' Then he turns back to the bloke with me and says, 'Hope she'll be all right, now — good luck to ye.' Then he disappears into the hedge.

"I tell you, the sweat was fairly running off me by the time we got to the phone. I had trouble enough dialling and my mouth was so dry I could hardly get the words out."

"I wouldn't worry that much — sure, they all know each other up there."

"I'm damn sure they knew each other — but they weren't going to let on, not with me around — I suppose if it had been you they might not have minded."

"If it had been me, they'd have known the car and kept out of the way — up there, they know you've got a new car before you've found out where the wiper switch is. You were just a stranger on their pad — they'll know you next time."

"There'll be no f — ing next time."

But house officer pay was poor enough — and there was.

★ ★ ★

There's a saying about truth coming from the mouths of babes and sucklings; just occasionally you can add "madmen". An urgent call, to a spot not too far from our locum's adventure, had me hurrying up there one night to be greeted by one of those scenes that you think only appear in poor-quality horror films.

The door was opened before I knocked — they'd been watching, waiting for me. I went into the main room and realised that all the furniture had been pushed roughly up to the walls as if the room had been cleared for a dance. And in a sense it had; the whole family (plus, I think, friends, neighbours and the local curious) were standing round against, or in some cases behind, the furniture. The dance floor was monopolised by a man of about seventy or eighty, shouting wildly and angrily at the top of his voice. So far, so straightforward — acute psychosis, origin to be determined. What made it a touch more awkward was that he was brandishing a meat cleaver with a vigour that effectively deterred any physical approach. One of the women, I presumed a daughter, made to remonstrate with him and was rewarded by finding the cleaver a good bit closer to her vital parts and shaken about with enough inaccuracy to turn alarm into panic.

I backed off towards the doorway, tugging at the sleeve of the chap who'd opened the door to me.

"How long's he been like this?" I asked in a near-whisper.

"He's not been himself this past few days, but this business only started tonight."

I attempted to strike up a conversation with the axe-man, with no result that was in any way relevant. In the middle of it, however, he began to tell tales of goings-on in the house in the days of the Troubles — just which Troubles I wasn't at first sure, for he was old enough to have been an adult at the time of the Easter Rising and to have had a hand in everything since — but the rant soon spread into a diatribe about one of our local colleagues who had "Been in with the Boys in the Cause". Madman's rant or not, there was a ring of truth in the detail of the disclosures, confirmed by the communal intake of breath from the assembly, whose every eye had swivelled round onto me to see the reaction — after all, this was dangerous territory and a word from me could have had them answering some very awkward questions in uncomfortable places.

I looked at my companion, shrugged my shoulders and said, "Ach, he's doting away there." The response was palpable relief all round and all was sweetness and light — at least as far as the extraordinary circumstances allowed.

We eventually got the old boy settled, disarmed and transferred to the local psychiatric unit. I see the family now and again — they're always grateful and often I get a broad smile, with a "knowing" element in it, at the end of a consultation — though I haven't been to the house since.

Not all such problems are so easily coped with. In the middle of a busy surgery, just when you can least afford to be interrupted, a call came through to my desk (I tried to screen all requests for visits when running single-handed); this one I couldn't put off, for it came from the Fire Brigade HQ.

"There's a fire at Ballylargan and we believe there's a person inside who needs your help."

"OK, I'll be there directly," said my voice, while a deeper inner voice said, "Why the hell don't you just ring for an ambulance — what do you think I'm going to do?" I gathered up the kit, made my apologies to the well-filled waiting room and headed out to the townland. As townlands go, Ballylargan is a small one and it was easy to see where the action was: two police cars, a fire engine and lots of people in uniform, together with a knot of onlookers, all shooed to a safe distance by the cops.

The centre of the scene was one of a group of so-called workers' cottages — plain, rendered, two-up, two-down places of a style found all over the Province. What made this one different was that it had lost a good chunk of its roof, all its windows were broken and both their frames and the front door itself were thoroughly charred black.

"Hello, Doc," shouted one of the cops. "You'd need to be careful going in there, now!" With this, he slid into the car and headed off.

"Hello, Doctor," shouted one or two of the firemen — they were all part-timers and all on my list — as they rolled up their hoses and stowed them onto the engine. "Watch how you go, mind — she'd wild!" Whereupon, loading finished, they too set off for base.

So there I was, on my own except for the spectators (who weren't going to be any help anyway), not knowing who, or for that matter what, I was to confront. I cautiously pushed open what was left of the door; the inside was dark and strikingly wet, water from the fire brigade's activities still pouring through the ceiling to form puddles on what had once been the tatty old carpet.

This much came at a glance, for a glance was all I got before being riveted by the object of the call. A huge, indeed mountainous, woman came forward to occupy much of my field of vision. She'd have made four or five of me (five foot three and size ten) and her attitude didn't encourage confrontation as she lumbered, wild-eyed and shouting, in my direction. She was indeed "wild" — in an episode of acute psychosis, she'd set the house on fire and then taken a carving knife to those who had come to help. She still had the knife in her hand — another discouragement to confrontation.

Devoid of all support, I adopted a tactic I'd never had to resort to before — I turned and fled; even without the knife there was no mileage to be gained in argument with this lassie. Momentarily I wished for the veterinary answer to this sort of situation — a blowpipe and a tranquillising dart — but without that, retreat was the only option.

Back outside, I collared one of the onlookers: "You just keep an eye on her from here in case she does anything silly, while I go and find a phone." Well, they'd had their bit of the circus — now it was time to throw one of them into the ring.

"Er . . . all right, Doctor." He was one of mine and knew better than to try to wriggle out of it, though I could see he suddenly wished himself elsewhere.

I found a phone and rang for the ambulance. "You'll need police assistance, it's more than a crew could handle on their own," I warned them. "The local boys know about this anyway, so there'll be no problem, I reckon." I tried not to chuckle audibly until I'd put the phone back on its rest. The cops weren't going to like this, but it was one of their official roles and they *had* run out on me, after all.

As luck had it, it was the police who arrived first and the same pair who'd been so keen to depart when I turned up.

"She's settled a bit, now, is she?"

"Not one bit — I think she's worse than ever and she's still got that knife."

This fairly wiped the confident smile off his face.

"Oh, f . . . Oh dear; did you not get her settled, then?"

"I couldn't get near her, not on my own — I had nobody with me, remember?" I made the remark as pointed as I could and smiled inwardly as I saw it sink home.

A combination of cajoling and *force majeure* eventually got her into the ambulance, leaving me free to return to the well-filled waiting room, hoping that with a bit of luck they'd all have got sick of waiting and gone home — but they hadn't.

61

At the beginning of the last bout of "Troubles" there was a phase when both sides to the conflict took to setting up unofficial roadblocks; these were usually at night in situations where the fellows concerned could melt away into the pitch-dark fields on the arrival of any force more official than theirs and be home at their firesides before the police had even got out of their cars.

By then, of course, we were both well-known familiar figures on the roads of the "patch" and were always greeted with an affable, "Go on ahead, Doctor — don't you mind all this, ye're OK now!" And on we would drive with a wave and a grin — after all, they were nearly all our patients and never for a minute did we feel in any way threatened or uncomfortable. On one occasion in a staunchly Republican area, I was stopped by one of these unofficial blockades and accosted by a figure in a black balaclava (black balaclavas were *de rigueur* fashion accessories for the Hard Men at that time), who asked me, in a rather hostile manner and an accent from at least a hundred miles south of where we were, who I was and what I was doing there. Before I could answer, a similarly masked figure tugged urgently at his sleeve and said something in his ear. The change was dramatic — with all the friendliness for which the Irish are renowned, he leaned forward, his eyes smiling through the slits of the mask, and said, "Sorry, Doctor, didn't know who you were — Oi'll know you for next time, sure." And sure enough, on the return trip half an hour later (how they hadn't been dispersed by then I couldn't fathom out), I got a wave as I swept through without even slowing down.

Gordon was a big bloke, burly with it, and never averse to a punch-up of a Saturday night once he'd put a few pints away. At other times he was a perfectly reasonable steady wage earner with a wife and a couple of growing kids to keep. A staunch Loyalist, the interior of his council semi was decorated with Loyalist symbols to leave the visitor in no doubt of where the attachments of that particular establishment lay; as the "Marching Season" approached, the house, like almost all of its neighbours, extended the décor to the outside, where it spilled onto the street in a riot of Red, White and Blue.

Small wonder then that his village, peopled by many of his persuasion, was often the scene of impromptu roadblocks at times when tensions rose, although on this day it was a bit out of the ordinary in that it was not on a pitch-dark night but on a warm Saturday afternoon in August. (Well, you can't take time off work just to set up a roadblock, now, can you?)

The confounding factor this time was that we had changed the car only a day or two beforehand. A call to the village saw me sweep around the bend into it, to be confronted by a group of the village worthies manning their checkpoint. It was apparent that this arm of the organisation was strapped for cash (unlike its always well-funded Republican counterpart) — no black balaclavas here; recognition was foiled by the cheaper expedient of pulling a woman's stocking over the face and head.

As a disguise, a 15-denier nylon stocking stretched over a familiar face leaves a lot to be desired: it only delays recognition by a millisecond or two and Gordon's build would have made him easily recognisable to anyone who knew the village. But Gordon, unsurprisingly, didn't know the car and waved me down with a swaggering imperiousness, well-practised from his Saturday nights. As soon as I wound down the window, of course, he knew me, but I couldn't resist the advantage that surprise gives you.

"Hey, Gordon," I called out, before he'd had time to form a response. "I hope you'll buy the wife a new pair of tights — she'll hardly be fit to wear those again, the way you've cut them!" For cut them he had, and in a hurry too, by the look of it: part of the gusset, still attached, flapped around his shoulder, betraying its origins only too clearly; better still (for me, anyway), only the broader part of the garment was wide enough to pull over his large face — the footpiece flapped and dangled off the crown of his head like some exotic top-knot. Had he had hair to stuff it with, he might just have got away with it; as it was, it very effectively turned the menacing to the ridiculous. Under the 15-denier, the face slowly turned scarlet — after all, you don't want your doctor to see you like this: you might have to undress for him some day and it could make dignity even harder to maintain.

"Oh . . . aye . . . er . . . it's you, Doctor . . . new car, is it?"

"It is, Gordon . . . but you'll know it for next time, won't you?" I felt I'd taken as much mileage as was reasonable from this and could safely leave the rest to his mates, who all seemed to be deriving a fair bit of amusement out of the encounter — they'd take it on from there, I had no doubt.

Neither of us ever referred to the matter again in all the times I saw the family — some things are better glossed over.

CHAPTER
SIX

Basic Instincts 1

Annie was neither bad nor mad; it was just that life had dealt her a rather poor hand. To call her attractive would have broadened the definition of the term and she made little effort to make the best of what nature had endowed her with. Invariably grubby, seriously overweight and with a permanent odour about her gathered from years of the unwashed state and an unhealthy closeness to the denizens of the farmyard who knew of no division between their domain and hers, you'd have expected her to have fallen at the first fence in the race to find a mate. She was, however, an affable soul and had about her — you could almost call it a charm — the natural courtesy of the isolated countrywoman. Isolated indeed she was: she lived "two fields in" from a tiny country lane in what once might have been a respectable, if modest, farmhouse but which had long been unfit for habitation by any "official" standards. She shared this four-crumbling-walls-and-leaking-roof with an aged father (at least we assumed he was her father — relationships get complicated out in the country, sometimes to the point where it's better not to enquire too closely). Apart from the livestock, the only other inhabitants of this ménage were five small children, about as close together in ages as children can be without being twins or whatever. This was the nub of the problem — her affability was of the "can't say 'No' " variety and as far as we could gather the children were the result of short-lived relationships with — well, possibly anyone who came along. Those who did come along didn't stay; Father had an interest in keeping her around as a maid of all work to support him in his old age and no doubt showed his unwillingness to approve of anything which might remove that support. One suitor, obviously keener than the rest, had defied the old man's displeasure and had had his persistence rewarded with the contents of both barrels of Daddy's shotgun as he fled for cover. We never quite understood how the old boy was allowed out and about again so soon, although it must be said that they wouldn't let him keep a gun any more after that.

Their only contact with civilisation (the village about four miles away) was at weekends when the two of them would go down on the tractor, a little grey Ferguson which Father drove while Annie stood on the axle and hung on to whatever she could. Once the shopping was done they would return the same way and not be seen again until next week, if then.

There was no point in trying to get Annie to come to the surgery for anything — her obstetric history was awful and antenatal care was usually confined to shipping her off to hospital as an obstetric emergency, for labour seemed to come as just as much of a surprise to her as it did to us, although at least we had the excuse of not knowing she was pregnant, for after all we didn't see her round the town often enough to miss her when she went to ground. This was a pity, for she was grossly obese and seriously hypertensive, while compliance with several attempts to institute a workable drug regime had been non-existent.

The children were not by any means unloved, but Annie's ability to manage them was just not there; indeed, the ability to manage a cat would have strained her cerebral resources. They ran, or crawled, or lay around in the area that one could at a pinch call the kitchen, always seeming in closer relationship to the four-footed occupants than to their mother, gathering immunity to all the local pathogens as they did so. Social Services, then fairly newly formed as a discipline and keen to show itself as important, if not vital, in the Survival of Mankind, held up its collective hands in horror when it found out about the household and set out on a "Something Must be Done" mission. The emissaries of this mission rarely got further than the door, for even without his gun Father had a way of discouraging unwanted visitors, and running back over two fields of quagmire to get to the safety of the car does nothing for one's confidence. So once again it was left to us and it seemed that the first thing to do was to try to make her accept some sort of contraception. She had no scruples about it; in fact, she had no opinion on the matter at all: "If you think that's best, Doctor" was about the height of her involvement.

I spoke to her father: short on the trigger he might have been, but at least he had a fair working idea of what I was trying to do. I suspect that his main concern was that, with no more pregnancies, Annie would be around more to look after him without all those annoying interruptions as yet another mouth to feed came into his world. He willingly lent his weight and influence to getting Annie to acquiesce to some form of contraception.

The question then was, what sort of contraception? There was no possibility that Annie would remember to take any regular oral preparation (the first "Pill" was just coming onto the market, although it had not yet begun to work the massive change in society which it brought about in later years, while injectable hormonal contraception was still decades in the future). Although we didn't realise it at the time, it was probably a good thing for Annie that we didn't try her on it, as she had what later came to be recognised as several major contraindications to its use and could well have been in serious trouble with it. The only other realistic option was a "coil", or intra-uterine device. These have been known from ancient times (the Arab masters of camel trains would insert a stone into the camel's uterus to avoid pregnancy on a long-haul caravan run), but at this time only one "medical" device was available (sticking pebbles into your patient's uterus was greatly frowned upon even then and would have probably seen you having to explain your actions to an unsympathetic GMC).

I had attended, not long before this, one of the early courses on fitting and usage of this device and felt Annie would be the perfect candidate for it. Then came the first snag.

"I can't go to no clinic in the town — sure, how am I to be getting there with all the weans an' me miles from the place?"

Various suggestions were made and rejected with a speed that made us feel that Annie was beginning to have cold feet over the idea. I'm still not sure how I came to be so foolhardy, but somehow I found my offer to fit her with it at home (an offer made in desperation and in the near-certain belief that it would be turned down) accepted with enough keenness to make backtracking impossible.

Maureen, the district nurse responsible for Annie's patch, responded to my tale with a long silence and a stare of disbelief. "You're not going to do that — out there, Doctor — surely?" That was all she said, but the effect, like a douche of cold water, made me realise that my triumphant glow of success was maybe a touch premature.

"You'll give me a hand, now, won't you?" I found myself almost wheedling support out of her. She knew me well enough to speak her mind and was as loyal as anyone could be; besides, anything that reduced the infant population of Annie's place could only lessen her load a bit, so she allowed herself to be dragged into it — "Though mind, Doctor, I'm not saying it's a good idea, y'know."

By then I was coming round to her way of thinking and wishing I'd kept my mouth shut and persuaded Annie to come somewhere, anywhere, more appropriate.

We arranged to do the job at the end of the regular day's work: unfortunately, of course, Sod's Law is always waiting to swing into effect and that day was a particularly busy one. A November dusk was drawing down as we set off and we would have missed the lane end, had Maureen not spotted it in the gloom.

We left the car at the field gate, gathered our kit and pushed the half-wrecked metal gate open — it took both of us to shift it.

"Just as well I came," Maureen grunted, as we heaved on it. She was right — I would not have wanted to start the job by having to climb over a gate which, however resistant to opening it was, looked incapable of bearing even my eight and a half stones. As we trudged into the first field, the coldness of the wet mud sloshing around my ankles increased the feeling that this was all going to go horribly wrong: I cursed myself for ever having thought of the madcap idea in the first place.

Annie's dad was there to greet us; his voice "had a smile in it" as he opened the door to us. We were too far away for him to hear Maureen mutter, "I bet he spoke like that just before he shot at that poor lad: it'd be just like him to lead us on into his trap."

Sometimes Maureen was inclined to let her imagination run away with her, but there was something spooky about the place even in daylight — in the dark it lost nothing of its eeriness.

What it did lose in the dark was light. I'd always been there in daylight with the door open and only now realised that not only was there was no electricity in the place but there was no source of light beyond candles. Many places were devoid of mains electricity but even if they didn't have a generator they nearly all had some reasonable means of lighting. Not so here — it was candles or nothing. No, this had not been a good idea.

Between us we explained (again) to Annie what we intended to do; she flopped onto the bed and rolled down her knickers, displaying yet another area that was a stranger to ablution. Several comments, all wholly improper, were stopped at the lips as we pondered how we might get to see what we were doing. A pen torch, when tried, confirmed our expectation that it was useless on its own.

"I've one of those big torches in the car," said Maureen. "Shall I go and bring it?"

She squelched off into the night, returning with a mansized lantern. "George always says I should keep a good powerful torch in the car when I'm out at night so much."

"Good idea," I said, mentally promising George a big kiss when I saw him at the Christmas party.

The torch made a big difference, though it fell far short of surgery lighting levels. Having worked our way to Annie's vital bits (easier said than done because of her massive obesity, although we encouraged ourselves with the thought that, as Maureen put it, "it's hardly an untrodden path, is it?"), I was able to insert a speculum. Now the pen torch came into its own.

"Hey, I can see the cervix!" I said, rather too loudly for the circumstances. I had a large area of flabby thigh against each cheek, my nose was where I'd have preferred it not to be and my glasses were steaming over, but this was triumph. The rest was easy, and in a few moments Annie was hauling her knickers back up and smiling.

"There, now, that wasn't too bad, now, was it?" We were all smiling now, just then Daddy came back into the room bearing a huge hissing paraffin lantern. It lit the place up like daylight, but it had taken him all the time we'd been working to pre-heat it and fire it up. You could see why candles were an easier option.

Oddities of reproductive life weren't confined to the General Practice side of our lives; the hospital's open-door policy brought a lot of them in there as well.

A large, seriously unkempt woman of — well, mature years shambled into the waiting room in the middle of a busy morning. At that time resources didn't stretch to having clerical staff in the department and first contact was with the nurse who combined the duties of Only Nurse with those of Receptionist and Triage officer; in other words, Dogsbody. She was first point of contact for this soul, and noted the yellowing hair, the slightly wild-eyed look and the well-weathered grey overcoat, its buttons stretched to their limits by the size of its contents.

Her question, "Well, now; what seems to be the trouble?" produced the reply, "I've seen nothing for three months — and there's something jumping about inside!"

Nurse's response was instant: "The antenatal clinic's over the road, dear; just go out the door again and turn right, then it's facing you."

She left and Nurse congratulated herself on her expeditious management, as well as on having reduced the queue by one with so little effort. We thought no more about it until the end of the morning, when the phone rang: it was the Obstetrician. His voice was just a little cooler than usual: "You sent a woman over to the clinic this morning."

"Er, yes — it was hard to get a clear story from her, but we assumed she was one of yours."

He started to laugh (when a colleague starts laughing at you down the phone, you know you've made an idiot of yourself, even before you get the details). "She wasn't pregnant at all, y'know."

"Really? What was it then?" I asked, trying to think of conditions that could produce the same history, and failing.

"She's just barking mad; she comes here from time to time with the same story, but she must have given up on us and gone to you today. You'll probably see her again before long!"

Other episodes aren't quite so funny, except in retrospect.

A late-night call from one of our more remote GPs caught me on a night when I was covering for the Gynae S.H.O. (Senior House Officer), paying back a favour. Things had been quiet — a bitterly cold spell had brought snow and ice which had half-melted then frozen again before further snow had fallen on it; it was not a night to encourage travel.

"There's a young woman having a bad haemorrhage up in Slaghtmore — you'll need the Flying Squad for her, she's losing a lot of blood."

I had taken the call myself. "What's her name?" I asked.

"Philomena Doherty — you'll need to come quick, now."

"What directions do I give . . .?" but she had already hung up.

John was duty driver that night; we woke him up and told him.

"Hope you got the directions all right, 'cos that's a big townland an' it's full of Dohertys and half the women in it are Philomenas."

I told him the story.

"I'll lay you money she hasn't been out there, especially on a night like this. Still, we'll need to go, even if she didn't."

By now the rest of the Flying Squad — a nurse, the driver's mate (a new chap called Sean, whom we'd hardly met) and myself — were climbing into a freezing cold ambulance and heading out of the hospital gates. We hit the ice immediately and our first two hundred yards or so, down the hill from the hospital to the town, were accomplished at an angle to our direction of travel which varied wildly from nought to forty-five degrees as

John struggled to keep the vehicle (never the best of road-holders even in the dry) on course.

"You'd have thought they'd have gritted this bit at least, for hospital traffic, tonight," I muttered.

"Damned apt!" John was too busy keeping off the pavements to comment more fully — besides, there was a lady present and John was of that generation that minded what he said when ladies were present. His face said plenty, however.

". . . and getting there's only the start of it; we could be on half the night finding her even when we get there."

Sean had been silent so far but then chipped in. "Where are we going, anyway?" he asked.

"Place called Slaghtmore, miles out in the hills, far from civilisation. Have you heard of it?"

"Heard of it? Sure, I live in Slaghtbeg, the next townland. Know it like the back o' my hand." His voice took on an aggrieved tone. "An' let me tell you, it's a very civilised wee place; they're all very decent up there."

"Oh, aye?" said John, "I mind one time . . ." He broke off, no doubt recalling the presence of the nurse. "Maybe tell ye later," he murmured.

It took an age to get to where the road towards the townland took off from the minor road, itself a couple of miles from what passed for the main road.

"It's a Philomena Doherty, but there's a lot of them up here," said John. "She'd be a youngish lassie, I reckon, if she's having a miss."

The road was piled with frozen snow down the centre, the trenches of tyre tracks on either side being sheet ice. Being seven or eight hundred feet up in the hills wasn't helping, either; the road was steeply graded and every yard posed a challenge to John just to keep us out of the ditches.

Sean pointed left: "There's a Philomena Doherty in there, but it'll hardly be her — she was telling my mother about her hot flushes three years or more ago so I think she'd be past it."

A few hundred yards further on, Sean gestured right. "There's a Philomena in the house at the back of that one, on down the lane a bit — but her husband's been away a while and she's sleeping out, so she'll be looking after herself."

"Where's her husband then?" I asked. "He wouldn't need to come back unexpectedly."

"He won't," said Sean confidently.

"Is he in England, then?" I asked.

"No — he's in the Crumlin — ten years — armed robbery. He'll hardly be home unexpectedly, now."

This silenced us for a few moments, then John spoke up.

"There's a light on — who lives there, Sean?"

"That could be her, now — she's about thirty, though she's not married — not that that signifies these days. I'd try there."

We stopped at the gate and tramped up to the door through a foot or more of virgin snow: no one had been here in the last few hours, that was for sure.

A middle-aged woman opened the door to us. "She's stopped now, Doctor, but she's lost an awful lot of blood."

This sounded a bit odd; miscarriages don't often stop like that, but we crowded into the tiny living room.

The target of all our efforts was sitting in a chair in front of the fire, a large, heavily bloodstained, towel wrapped around her face and neck — hardly the place to put a towel to mop up a miscarriage. What we could see of the rest of her seemed quite normal, at that distance anyway.

The towel came down as we entered the room, revealing a bloodstained face, mainly around her chin and mouth. As she unwrapped herself, she coughed up a lump of blood clot and caught it on the towel.

John's mouth was close to my ear and I heard him mutter, to himself rather than to me, "Would ye f — ing well believe it? To come out with a Flying Squad for a f — ing nosebleed!"

It was as well I was the only one in earshot as John's principles went by the board.

Her mother spoke up. "We rang for the doctor, but she said the roads were too bad to come out and she'd send an ambulance." Neither she nor, apparently, the doctor had seen anything incongruous in this remark — after all, to them the ambulance wasn't subject to the laws of weather, or for that matter the laws of physics, and could materialise out of thin air whatever the circumstance — *deus ex Machina* indeed!

We hadn't come equipped for nosebleeds, but it looked like one that could start up again and we didn't fancy another trip out on a night like this. We suggested that she should come down with us "to get it properly dealt with," a suggestion which was accepted as if no other action could ever have been contemplated.

Mind you, she had to make her own way home the next day; one trip like that is enough.

CHAPTER
SEVEN

Basic Instincts 2

As in the rest of the world, the other basic instinct that keeps life turning is the making of money and, here anyway, keeping it from the eyes of the Revenue. Many's the small farmer who goes through life ill-dressed, living in near-squalor and denying himself any half-decent standard of living, just so that he can amass a collection of cash; usually all he does with it is to pass it on to a less-than-grateful family who promptly spend it.

Joe, a GP from about twelve miles away, rang in the middle of a morning ward round.

"I wonder if you'd take in an old boy for me — I've been trying to get him to agree to come to you for nearly a week, but he always refused point-blank to be moved; today he's too ill to argue. It looks to me as if he's got a fulminant pneumonia; in fact, he looks like someone who's not going to do."

An hour or two later he was brought in, a bundle of rags on the ambulance trolley, pale and fighting for breath with what little strength was left to him. Oxygen and an intravenous line seemed to make him a shade more comfortable, although he was in no condition to speak, let alone give a coherent story: this came from one of his daughters, a perfectly normal, respectably dressed woman of forty or so, who looked a bit out of step with our patient. The story explained the incongruity; he'd always been a difficult character to live with — the local word "thrawn" summed him up, possibly too kindly — and he had been abandoned by his family, one by one, as they made their own lives without him. They'd rallied round him when this illness had struck, blood being always thicker than water, but even their efforts added to those of the GP had been unavailing in getting him to acquiesce to hospital admission.

Hurried investigations revealed more than just a pneumonia — he had a gross septicaemia with what today we would call "multiple organ failure" (although I don't think the term was in use at that time) and whatever we did for him, at this stage he was doomed. His family took this news with equanimity (I suspect they might have been a mite relieved that they weren't going to have him as a dependent at home to inflame all the old hostilities).

It took him only eighteen hours to fulfil our predictions and slip away before we even had the bacteriology results to hand. As one does, we got on with the business of treating the living and put him out of our minds, or at least out of the forefront of our minds.

It was almost a week later, while I was talking to Joe on another matter, that he said, "You remember my old boy with the septicaemia last week? Well, we found out why he was so reluctant to leave that awful hovel. The family were clearing out the place and nearly everything in it was fit only for burning. So they had this bonfire going in the farmyard and dragged everything out — clothing, furniture, everything that could possibly burn. When it came to the mattress they were just pulling and pushing it onto the blaze with bits of poles, because it was so awful they didn't even want to touch it, when one of the sticks tore the side of the mattress and a pound note fell out. So instead of burning it straight away, they tore off the cover and — guess what?"

"A couple of hundred quid fell out?" I ventured.

Joe laughed. "Couple of hundred, you say? In that filthy old heap they found ... *twenty-six thousand pounds* in notes!"

I gasped; after all, at that time five thousand pounds would have bought you a decent detached house and probably left enough over to buy a car as well. What he could have done with twenty-six thousand was in the realm of fantasy.

"Didn't do him much good, did it?"

"No," said Joe, "though I suppose it could get him a better coffin. Not that the family'll buy one for him, though — they'll have other things to spend it on."

Central to keeping your cash tax-free is the perceived need to have it around you at all times. Keeping it in the mattress was the commonest way of cosying up to it; at least you could count it to help you off to sleep. But there were other ways of having it handy.

"Collapse coming in from the market yard — about five minutes." The message from switchboard was brief but gave all the information needed, or indeed available, at that moment.

"These ould farmers are all the same; they get over-excited when they're bidding and get into bother," said staff nurse, as we prepared to receive him. "He'll either be dead or rarin' to get back to the sale."

This one was very firmly in the latter group, sitting up on the ambulance trolley and protesting loudly: "Sure it was just a wee dwam — I'm rightly now, so I am."

Clinical examination from a distance tended to support his contention, but attempts to remove his clothing for a proper look provoked marked resistance, almost amounting to panic.

I tried reasoning. "I can't let you go until I've checked you over — if there's nothing to be found we'll get you away quick as you like." The authority of the white coat eventually won him over and very reluctantly he undressed, removing a large, very heavy and dirt-encrusted overcoat, a jacket, a waistcoat, a flannel shirt badly in need of washing, a pair of muddy Wellington boots and an equally muddy pair of trousers tied with string. His concern seemed to be directed exclusively to the overcoat, to which he devoted his constant attention.

Unfortunately our initial optimism about getting him home took a fatal knock when an ECG tracing revealed unequivocal evidence of his having had a small heart attack. If he'd protested at being examined it was nothing to the protesting he did when we told him he'd need to come into hospital. Eventually we managed to persuade/threaten/scare him into agreement and the girls began documenting his possessions as part of the admission process. His agitation grew sharply as they came to check the contents of his overcoat. The reason for the agitation and for the undue heaviness of the coat soon became apparent; the lining seemed remarkably thick but a hand stuck into one of the several tears in it brought out a bundle of twenty-pound notes (items rarely seen at that time).

"How much have ye got in there?" said Staff, increasingly wide-eyed as she fished out bundle after bundle of ten- and twenty-pound notes from the recesses of the lining. "Ye'd get a quair few head o' cattle wi' all that!" By the time we'd made sure that the old coat had been wholly denuded of its contents, we had nearly ten thousand pounds sitting on the table beside him, an amount such that the Deputy Matron had to be called to verify and sign for it before transporting it to the hospital safe. Judging by the look on our patient's face, the formal hospital receipt for the cash was no substitute for having it actually in his grasp; I felt it might even jeopardise his recovery to be parted from his beloved money.

Things only got worse when it was pointed out that we couldn't keep this sort of sum, even in the safe, and that he would have to get a relative to take it away. Hearing this, his agitation reached new heights and we began to fear for his wellbeing. When the "Appointed Relative" turned up, we began to understand at least some of his concerns. Stocky, equally unkempt, he had, in Staff Nurse's words, "The sort o'leer that told you just where that money'd be going — and it wouldn't be to any bank, I'll be bound!"

"If that went to a bank, it'd be the first time those notes have seen one since they were printed!" was my only comment.

Despite our reservations, our patient did recover fully; how he got on with the "Appointed Relative" (who was probably disappointed to see him walk out of hospital alive and well), history does not record — and it's probably just as well.

Other ways of saving money are much more laudable and in today's climate are vigorously encouraged even by governmental policy now that energy saving has become not only respectable (it always was in my eyes), but essential. As is often the case, many an Ulster farmer was there first, but kept it to himself.

Ireland generally and Ulster in particular — at least that's how it feels — is wet, its generous ration of rain filling the rivers and streams of the Province and making it green. Some of the attraction of the "green" can wear off when you're driving through sheeting rain and long roadside pools of water (or "soil solution", as I've called it at times), or walking unexpectedly across fields of well-stirred mud.

But to the fortunate few, water means power. It's the sort of thing you don't notice in the daily round and it's not part of the usual history-taking. My first encounter with this phenomenon was on a call to see a small child way out in the country at an old mill in one of that multitude of vignettes of great beauty that characterises the Province — always well-hidden from the through traffic, in wooded valleys or nestling in the fold of a hill, they can be a delight as much from their unexpectedness as for their intrinsic attractiveness.

The mill was in use as a sawmill and derived its power from the river beside it; a century or so earlier a dam had been thrown across it and virtually the whole flow diverted through a turbine (the old wooden water wheel is strictly for the calendar pictures), which not only powered the saw but, as I was to learn, drove an ancient generator to light and heat the house.

I stopped in the forecourt and got out of the car. The house looked quite shut up, but the noise from the big shed beside it indicated activity; I made my way over to it, impelled by curiosity as much as the need to ask the way in.

My arrival had gone unnoticed against the noise in the building and I was able to stand and watch for a while before making my presence known. A tall, well-built man of forty-odd was feeding a large baulk of timber into the teeth of a huge circular saw which was steadily and noisily chewing its way through it, scattering sawdust and particles of wood around as it did so. What grabbed my attention, however, was the sight of a six-inch-wide flat belt hurtling across the floor at about adult shin height, traversing the full width of the shed, nipping around the pulley on the saw spindle and flying back whence it came, into some deep recess at the side, from which came a steady hum interspersed with the rhythmic slap of the belt joint as it whizzed onto the pulley. A gaggle of small children were playing around in the shed; two of the older ones were jumping to and fro over the flying belt in a variant of skipping — although the penalty for getting it wrong was way beyond anything you'd get from a skipping rope: the prospect of being swept up in the belt, flayed between the outward and inward bound lengths before being carried off to the river or the sawbench must have been a great stimulus to get it right first time, every time.

I am no lover of the Health and Safety fascists who nowadays hedge about our every activity with "Thou Shalt Not", but I felt even at first glance that this state of affairs left a fair bit to be desired. The kids had seen me and stopped their suicidal play to attract Father's attention.

"She's in the house, Doctor — ye'd need to go in the back way; the door's open." He returned to pushing in the timber baulk and I made my way to the house.

The house was comfortable and warm on a still-nippy spring day. I soon saw where the warmth was coming from; each room was heated by the simplest of means — in the corner stood an old electric cooker, its oven door off and all its switches turned on, taking the energy from the river. Not only frugal, but ingenious and, in today's parlance, the ultimate in environmentally friendly energy. In later visits I found him a source of good sound knowledge on the subject, knowledge that many another came to glean and make use of.

Another encounter was rather more dramatic; in the earlier days of the most recent "Troubles", we had a period of power cuts engendered purely as an exercise in political power-wielding. This gave us a daily series of power cuts at irregular hours, themselves a source of stories a-plenty. During one of these periods of blackout, a weekend call took me to the next town. It presented an eerie sight; in total darkness, save for a few scattered oil lamps and candles in windows, it gave one a perfect image of what the town would have looked like on such a night a hundred or more years ago. Until, that is, I turned the bend in the road and saw my destination. The place was lit up like the proverbial ocean liner — lights were on, it seemed, in every room in the house, while as soon as I got out of the car I could hear the sound of the television. What I couldn't hear was any sound of a motor generating set.

The consultation over, I raised an eyebrow to the man of the house, gestured to the lights, TV and electric heaters, all going strong, and said, "How come?"

His face lit up. "Are you interested?" he said. Taking my enthusiastic nod for assent, he led me out to the back of the house and into the back garden, one no different from any of its neighbours except for a more-substantial-than-average garden shed at the bottom. From this came a steady hum and over it I could hear the sound of water running. My guide opened the door (a much more robust one than would grace the average garden shed) and switched on the light.

A spinning shaft rising vertically out of the floor carried a pulley on it, from which the standard flat belt drove a generator, its output recorded on a pair of dials on the wall behind it.

"My father put this in before the war, but it fell into disuse until a few years ago when we set about fixing it all up again — we had a fair bit to do, but I had the generator rewound and it runs a good bit of the brother's place, just over there" — he gestured across the stream to a small farmhouse a field away — "and it's been well worth it, even before all this bother, now — wouldn't be without it."

A small stream which I'd passed many times almost without noticing was providing all the electrical needs of the house in a most inconspicuous way, cleanly and silently, day in, day out: as I left, I wondered just how many more of these there were in the country. To judge by the darkness of the rest of the town, though, this was the only one in sight tonight.

Like so much here, there's an awful lot going on out of sight.

CHAPTER
EIGHT

Fear

Fear, however well hidden, can be a potent source of medical work — indeed, you could say that it's an element of almost every contact made. In some people, however, it can be so well concealed that it passes unnoticed to all but the most searching eye.

Willy was one of those — a great bull of a fellow, whose behaviour to his wife and children would have disgraced a bull of any species. He lived on the edge of the practice, half an hour's run along the narrow twisting roads even if you found the place first time: as he called us out perhaps once every three years, if that, each journey was made anew and like as not incorporated the same wrong turnings as the previous trip.

The townland housed several of his brothers, all physically very similar and of much the same turn of mind, although Willy was certainly the worst of them: Bella, his wife, would turn up regularly at the surgery with black eyes and enough injuries to have had Willy on a charge of Grievous Bodily Harm twice over. But if intervention was suggested she was always horrified — and only partly because of the inevitable violent response it would set off. In some way her wretched self-effacing nature left her content, or at least resigned to being the target of her man's temper. If he ever felt remorse, maybe this was the only time she exerted any influence upon him. Faced with this situation, all you can do is to keep on offering help and be there to pick up the pieces.

One summer's day when I'd just begun to feel that life was going to be quiet for the next few hours, the phone rang. It was one of Willy's sisters-in-law in a rare state of panic. "Doctor, you'd need to come quick — Harry's ta'en a terrible bad head and now he's collapsed and isn't talking."

Not the sort of call you could fob off. Harry, a younger brother of Willy, was not as regular an attender as we would have liked — he had gross hypertension which he treated only intermittently, when he could bother to get a supply of tablets, and we'd worry about him when others of the tribe came in, or came to mind. But he had his fair share of the family obstinacy and J. had long ago given up trying to make him comply with advice. So often those who pride themselves on being tough as young men defy the advancing years by denying to themselves that any disease can ever touch them and Harry's neglect of himself was just another gesture of defiance at life.

I reached the house and saw that one or two people were standing around outside, while half a dozen cars were parked around the yard. This looked bad — folks don't gather like that for a headache and I already had a provisional diagnosis of a fatal sub-arachnoid haemorrhage as I got out of the car. The group regarded me with the sort of look that tells you everything; I raised an eyebrow in question and received a slow nod in reply. So, it was to be a matter of certifying death and dispensing comfort, if the platitudes of a relative stranger can be called comfort. This I knew before I was fully out of the car.

I went in with minimum ceremony. Harry lay on a table, already more or less laid out — the undertaker and a nurse each lived within a few hundred yards and had easily beaten me to the house as well as pre-empting the diagnosis. I murmured some sympathy to his wife, who stared wildly at me and cried out, "Ah, Doctor, is he gone? Is he really dead, is he, Doctor, is he?" I looked at the body on the table, a Bible tucked under his chin, clean pyjamas on and his hands folded across his chest. Resisting the urge to say, "Well, if he's not, what the hell's he doing lying like that?" I settled for the less contentious, "I'm afraid so." Still a bit wild-eyed, she took me by the hand and led me, puzzled, out of the house and round to the gable end away from the road, where oddments of household junk had been dumped over the years. She stopped among this between some lengths of chicken wire and an old piece of drainpipe and began to lift her dress. "My God, I'm going to be raped" was my first thought. My second was, "My God, she's going to claim I raped her!" Alarm was mounting when I realised, with some relief, that she was simply taking off one of her thick woollen stockings and wasn't in fact going to strip naked before me.

92

"Doctor, while you're here — I've been bothered with this leg of mine; it's been troubling me for months — d'ye think it'll be all right?" She showed me a leg not in too bad shape for its age, with a little cluster of varicose veins in one area.

So this was it — the route by which her fear had come to the surface. You can call it bizarre, which indeed it was, but there was the cry for help, for reassurance that she, at least, had more time allotted to her on this Earth. I gave the assurance with all the confidence I could show, then she put back on her stocking and we returned together to the house door, where I took my leave.

From this time on, we began to see more of Willy, although it was hard not to let one's hackles rise at the man — he was gruff to the point of rudeness, while Bella's visits, and bruises, became more frequent than ever.

On one of his first visits after Harry's death, we managed to get to take his blood pressure, something he'd managed to avoid for quite a few years by one ploy or another. I think he knew what was in our minds and knew that Harry's death was in some way linked to his blood pressure and it was certainly this which made him almost insufferable this day. His pressure was about 250/130; in other words, it was out through the roof, at a highly dangerous level. We had to tell him — there was no other way round this and it might at least frighten him into better compliance than his brother had shown. We let him in as gently as we could: "Willy, that pressure's not too bad now, but I think it's a bit on the high side; if we get it down a bit I think it would help your headache [his presenting symptom]."

"That's what *he* had, isn't it? *He* used to get headaches and him a man as never had ache or pain in his life, didn't he?"

For the first time I saw Willy frightened and took him gently: "Yes, I know, but his was worse than yours by far [it wasn't — it hadn't been in the same league], and besides, it's something we can help a lot."

His face twisted about, chewing on some phrase he wanted. "But — Ah've never ailed a thing in my life — see them hands?" He held up two shovel-like hands on wrists to match. "Ah've seen me lift nigh three hunnerweight and carry it across thon yard without stopping once, man." He shrugged, ever so slightly. "Mind you, that was when I was a younger man, now."

"Willy, we're all of us getting older and you can't expect to do that sort of thing now." He said nothing, but plainly resented his advancing years. He went out with a prescription and advice. Things must have been rough that night, for Bella was in the next morning, as knocked-about as ever we'd seen her.

Then something seemed to happen as he came back for reviews at intervals. His pressure came remarkably well under control — compliance was not going to be a problem here — but a change came upon him. The viciousness so near the surface even in the surgery seemed to retreat and his gruffness became that of an old countryman hiding some quality which could almost be affability. Certainly he smiled at times, an odd phenomenon indeed, and once he pressed a pound note into my hand in spite of my quite genuine protestations, for they were far from wealthy people. He even said "Thank you," words which must have been strange to his lips, but all the more valued for that.

He's kept going for a good few years now, rather to our surprise, and is remarkably well. I've even heard him crack a joke or two, although the very awkwardness of it was a joke in itself. I found myself beginning almost to like the man. His symptoms had settled, but with them had departed the fear that had surfaced as blind frustration, rage — and violence, for we saw Bella much less frequently; true, there was the odd weekend bust-up, but no more than many a couple in the practice would have had. If he'd turned all sweetness and charm — now *that* really would have had her worried! Willy can go on denying his years and his pathology — as long as he keeps on taking the tablets.

"Doctor, would you come and see Teresa some time today? She's got this pain back again and she's not well at all."

"Surely — I'll call in sometime today; just expect me when you see me," I replied.

There was a pause and the voice said, "There's a death in the family — but you wouldn't know, Doctor. It was her brother, but he wasn't a patient of yours. The funeral's this evening."

"Oh, I'm sorry; I didn't know. Was it sudden?"

"Well, sortaways, y' know, though he hadn't been well this long time."

"I'll come after the funeral, then — perhaps that would be best?"

"If that's all right with you, Doctor. Thanks."

The McCarthys were a nice family — a brother (now, it seemed, deceased) and two sisters, one married, the other, Teresa, a spinster in her fifties or thereabouts. She'd had odd problems from time to time, the main one being a renal infection which had eventually lost her one kidney, although she coped fine with her job as an office cleaner, cycling three or four hilly miles to work to contribute her bit to the housekeeping. I was happy to oblige them by going at a time of their choosing, for they never made any demands on us, soldiering on even when they should have been using the service, just getting on with life — and death.

The house, a quarter-mile or so from a tiny road, was on a site cut into the hillside. I suppose the next house beyond its back door would have been eight or nine miles of hill and moor away. There were five or six cars in the front yard — I was probably a bit too early for the ending of the formalities.

The interior was sparsely but tidily furnished and utterly spotless; I think that was how it always was, rather than having been done up for the wake. They were that sort of people.

On the table, incongruously genteel in the context of an old Ulster farmhouse, lay two large plates of cucumber sandwiches; thin-cut, the crusts all cut off, and laid out in neat circles, they wouldn't have been out of place in the tea tent at Henley or Wimbledon.

Sectors of cake, similarly arranged, caught my eye as I was ushered through to the stairway behind. The guests were obviously in the Front Room and hadn't reached the cucumber sandwich stage yet.

The bedroom, its ceiling sloping down to a small dormer window, was even more basic: apart from the bed, the one object that attracted notice was a grandfather clock. The clock itself was nothing startling — a country-made painted dial job, its case covered in layer upon layer of blackened, cracked varnish — but what took my eye (and my attention off the matter in hand) was that the clock was far too tall for the room. The Ulster farmer's usual solution to this is to cut off the base of the case to fit it in, but here he had simply cut a hole in the ceiling, through which the top of the clock simply disappeared into the darkness of the roof space, into which you had to peer to see the time.

I dragged my attention away from this to the bed and its occupant. Teresa lay on her side, half curled-up, her eyes just about open and her face the picture of misery.

"My sorrow for your trouble." I opened the conversation with the traditional greeting to the newly bereaved. A slight silent movement of the lips acknowledged the words. A pause, then the tears came. "Doctor," she sobbed, "I'm so sick — it's even worse than last time."

"When did this all start, then?"

"Just yesterday — I'd been trying to help with Johnny's [she sobbed and gulped again] wake and it came on so quick, I had to give up and lie down."

She was sore and tender, but not in the flank from which the kidney had been removed. The scar, an old one, was quiet and there was nothing to suggest that the problem lay there.

"You've got some infection somewhere but I don't think it's the old trouble again — have you any other bother?"

"No, just a bit of a cut on my knee where I fell off the bicycle last week."

Sure enough, under the bandage she'd applied was a dirty deep septic graze: a poke at the glands in her groin made her yelp, as much with surprise as pain.

"You know, I think this is coming from that cut — the poison's getting into the system and it's certainly got as far as those glands; I reckon that's all that's going on and a good whack of antibiotic'll sort you out in no time."

She looked at me, wide-eyed: "You really think so — really?" Her hand came out and clutched mine for confirmation.

"Sure I do — no point in lying to you, now, is there?"

She sobbed again, but it was different this time, more relief than misery. Then she began to speak of her brother and I saw that the call, though genuine enough, had a deeper, a far deeper cause, one I could hardly probe in these circumstances. She had suddenly been made aware of her own mortality by her brother's death and her own illnesses — and she was not coping with staring death in the face, even vicariously. What she needed was much more complex than mere physical treatment and probably more than I could hope to give by myself, but at least I might have begun the process of a healing of the spirit by leaving her relieved and relaxed.

I didn't see her again for years, then one day she turned up with a twisted ankle. She was so much changed I wouldn't have known her, had I not had the record card before me. The ankle was easy to sort out and as she left, she half-turned to me and said softly, "Thank you — so much."

I knew she didn't mean the ankle.

CHAPTER
NINE

Magic and Misery

It was in the middle of an ordinary morning that the phone rang.

"Ambulance is away out for an RTA. One injured — believed a cyclist. They should be in in about twenty minutes — OK?"

"Right-o, thanks." I passed on the details to the girls; they knew the routine and needed no more prompting — this, after all, was what we were there for and at least we could prepare as far as we could pending further details when the crew had got to the scene and assessed the situation. Radio contact was dependent on where you were and our area had its share of black (or should it be blank?) spots where radio silence reigned. All you could do then was to wait until the ambulance had crested the next rise in the ground and catch what you could of the message before it descended into the dip.

Time passed — there was no communication and a couple of calls to switchboard (where the only receiver was sited) drew blanks.

"Either he's dead or he's got up and run away," I muttered, more to myself than to anyone in earshot. We went on with the rest of the morning's work, rather than let a queue build up in anticipation of something that might turn out to be non-existent.

About an hour after the first call, wee Billy (one of the drivers stationed in the town nearest to the site of the incident) sidled in to the department and stuck his head around the door of the office. The black serge uniform seemed always to be a bit on the big side for wee Billy — unlike that of his larger namesake, whose buttons had some difficulty meeting as the years went on. He spoke softly out of the corner of his mouth so that only I could hear him.

"We've brought yer man in from the RTA. He's round the back, but there's nobody seen him yet — ye'd need to maybe nip round and check, Doc."

This was all quite irregular — if he hadn't been certified dead at the scene, he should really have been brought into the department for certification before being taken off to the mortuary, but I could trust the boys — the older hands anyway — to recognise death when they saw it: they'd seen plenty of it in their time. Nonetheless, I set off "round the back" directly; it was only a matter of fifty yards or so.

He lay on the mortuary table quite dead, his face as devoid of expression as it was when the lorry catapulted him off his bike into eternity. George, the mortuary porter, was already sorting him out, removing garments one at a time and going through the pockets looking for something to identify him by, for we still had no name for him. From the threadbare brown jacket he drew a stained cutty pipe, a half-consumed packet of tobacco,

101

a bottle of methylated spirit wrapped in brown paper and still intact in spite of the circumstances, a box of matches, then — two short lengths of twig, each about three inches long and each with both ends thoroughly charred.

"Ach, well, well, well," said George, "a charmer — wonder what it was that he had?"

I hadn't come across burnt twigs before, not in the pockets of the newly deceased anyway. I raised an eyebrow to George. "Tell me more," I said.

"He'd have had a charm to cure something or other — those'll be bits of willow cut at the right time of year and charred in a wood fire. When he'd be doing the cure, he'd draw a circle around the part in question and say a wee prayer over it and then it would get better."

"You mean he'd cast a spell on it?"

George looked at me from the corner of his eye, evidently not sure just where to steer the conversation.

"Aye, well, sort of — I suppose you could call it that," he said rather awkwardly, not sure if I was going to make fun of him: it seemed from the unspoken bit of the reply that he certainly didn't regard it as mumbo-jumbo. I was going to have to be diplomatic about it if I was to get very far. But it was too good an opportunity to pass up — a real magician here in the middle of the twentieth century among all the technology of the age: a survival of a system of belief going back beyond the medieval, probably to pre-Christian times and the age of the wise man and the Doctor-Priest.

I'd come across the work of the "Charmer" before often enough, though inevitably only when their efforts had failed; not so long before this I'd been consulted by a local businessman — not the sort of person to get worked up over the supernatural — who'd hobbled into the cubicle one morning with a very nasty-looking swollen ankle. His reply to the question "what happened?" elicited the story that he'd twisted it over a week ago. When it hadn't settled in a few days he'd gone off for a cure to one who had "The Charm For The Sprained Ankle". (It seems that Charmers are disorder-specific — no good taking your shingles to a Sprained Ankle man, then.)

"What did he do, then?" I asked, marvelling the while that someone like him had taken such an unconventional approach to treatment.

"Well, he got me to show him the ankle then he rubbed it all over with some sort of grease or fat; then he got out a wee stick of charcoal or something like that and drew a circle around the swelling while he said some wee prayer that I couldn't catch. He said it would be better in a week — but it's not, so I thought I'd maybe come and see what you thought of it."

It's always suitably humbling to know that you're second-best to the local witch doctor, but I tried not to be too smug as I came back from looking at his X-rays.

"I have the answer to your problem," I said, as po-faced as I could keep myself. "You should have gone to the man with The Charm For The Broken Ankle."

He had the good grace to laugh even louder than I would have dared to.

★ ★ ★

Charmers came in various sorts, some operating in a conventional, "clinical-consultation" context, others moving with the times and offering their services by telephone — a sort of "miracle for tuppence" arrangement that brought no profit to the miracle worker but at least saved time.

The other sort was more in the way of herbalists, playing their trade with variously noxious concoctions usually for surface use only. Having seen what they did to the surfaces, it was as well that they weren't taken internally, or they could have kept a team of general surgeons in employment for years. As it was, their victims provided material for training in basic plastic surgical techniques for a whole generation of junior staff.

Their speciality was the treatment of warts and growths of various sorts on the skin, all of which were designated as "Cancers", no doubt to encourage compliance with what was to be a painful procedure. The offending area would be covered with a patch of adhesive dressing onto which had been spread a mixture of mystery ingredients (rumoured to contain a large amount of arsenic compounds) and the patient sent off with strict orders to leave the patch alone until it fell off on its own. This must have been a difficult instruction to comply with, as the pain, initially at least, was agonising. Eventually, however, the patch would fall away, bringing with it all the underlying tissues; at best this left a deep scar, conspicuous and slow to heal; applied to the ear or the lip, however, it left a (usually large) defect. Many was the old man (men formed by far the greater part of this clientele) who sported an ear, a lip or even a nose with a large piece missing.

One such who came to our notice, referred by his GP after years spent trying to persuade him to have something done, presented with a huge loss of tissue from his lower lip; for over twenty years this had prevented him from swallowing properly and had forced him to drink lying on his back once the loss of his lower front teeth had removed the means of retaining fluid in his mouth. Surgery for this was of the simplest kind — an excision of the scar and stitching of the edges together; it wasn't elegant, but it allowed him to form a seal to his mouth for the first time in years. Even now, half a century later, I can still see the tears of gratitude on his face when he found he could once again eat and drink with dignity. The sadness was that he had, more than likely, borne all this unnecessarily — the original problem could well have been non-malignant and a small local removal with minimal residual deformity could have saved him years of misery. By comparison, trimming a well-nibbled piece of ear to a more socially acceptable shape was even smaller beer.

I made my way back towards my unit, still mulling over the extent of the influence of folk medicine and magic in this part of the world. As I swung around a corner of the corridor I almost collided with a woman coming slowly the other way. I opened my mouth to apologise then realised it was none other than Irene from the practice. Although I'd kept in touch with her progress over the years since our first encounter and had seen her once or twice, I hadn't clapped eyes on her for a few years by then.

"Hello, how are you keeping?" I said to her. "Are you up for a review then? How's the kidneys?"

She smiled, but not the fulsome smile I usually got from her.

"Oh, I'm not too bad now — well under control, as they say. No, I'm up with Colin — in fact I was hoping we'd be able to see you yourself, Doctor; I feel we can rely on you to sort him out." Considering the circumstances of our first encounter, this was praise indeed.

"What's been the trouble?" I asked with some concern. Colin was her eldest son and had just done his A levels with every prospect of a place at university. Like most boys of his age and stage he was not one to bother any doctor and I hardly knew him from personal contact, so this was likely to be significant.

"He's had this sore knee for a few weeks now and it's getting no better. Doctor J thought it was a sprain but, to be honest, Doctor, I'm worried about him; he says he didn't injure it at any time and — well, between you and me, he doesn't look all that well."

"Is he round in the department, 'cos I'm just on my way back there and I'll see him as soon as I can."

Colin didn't have too long to wait and his story was exactly as his mother had told it to me. There was some slight redness and tenderness, not in the knee but just

106

above it in the lowermost part of the thigh, with a suspicion of a fullness there. It was the wrong place for a joint inflammation, so more for the sake of completeness than with any expectation of finding anything, I arranged an X-ray of the area.

He had to wait a while for this, but was in the X-ray room as I was passing the door of the adjacent processing/viewing room. One of the radiographers beckoned to me, her face serious.

"This is that young lad you sent round," she said, gesturing to the film on the viewing screen. I moved in to look and felt a cold sickness inside me as I scanned the film. There was no mistaking the appearance — a huge area of bone effectively missing from the lower thigh, converted into swollen tumour mass. The pattern was all too diagnostic — this was an osteosarcoma, a highly malignant bone tumour and already far more extensive than would have been apparent clinically, even if it had been in the forefront of my mind rather than lurking dimly in the depths of unspoken intuition; perhaps it was that that made me go for the X-ray, an almost subconscious consideration of the possibility that hadn't quite made it into a fully formed thought.

"Oh, Christ, no!" was all that came from me as the vision of his next few years passed before me in seconds — amputation, chemotherapy, the inevitable eventual appearance of secondaries and a promising young life cut short, for the outlook for this was pretty grim. Sometimes the privilege of knowledge that Medicine brings can be uncomfortable indeed.

I took the films round to show them directly to the radiologist, in the faint hope that he might have an alternative diagnosis to offer.

"Would you glance at these and tell me I'm wrong — please?"

He put the films on his viewing screen: his intake of breath was as sharp as mine had been a minute earlier. Like myself, he had little doubt of the diagnosis. I told him the story and we sat silent for a few seconds.

"I'll do a report on that now — I imagine you'll want to send the films on with him straight away."

"Aye, once I've talked to him. Lord knows how I'm going to break this to him; I'll let him in gently but I'll need to talk to his mother — at least she knows me well enough to trust me."

Back in the department, Colin was safely out of the way in a cubicle and Irene was out in the waiting area. I beckoned her over and we moved out of earshot of the other occupants. (Dedicated space for interviewing relatives was still in the future at that time, although the need for it was becoming ever more pressing.)

"It's serious, isn't it, Doctor?"

She'd seen the look on my face and read enough into it to know that things were far from well.

"Irene, it's not so much serious — it's devastating".

I explained the situation as simply as I could, trying not to sound too pessimistic, although her face showed that she saw through my attempt to put the best prognosis on it — not that there's much of a "best prognosis" to offer in these circumstances.

"I can't tell him any lies, Irene, but I'm not going to tell him everything. I'll have to let him in a bit at a time, but the first thing is to get him to the Regional unit that deals with these and I'll organise that now."

A couple of phone calls had the transfer arranged and Irene, armed with referral letter and films (after the latter had been copied for the archives), took him off to the Unit. At least she knew the way, for she'd been a regular attender at one of the adjacent units for her kidney problem: after all that trailing up and down on her own behalf it seemed doubly unjust that she should now be ferrying her son who was far worse off than she'd ever been and who was almost bound to predecease her.

The day had become quite grey and my lively curiosity over the Magician and his likes was almost forgotten in an even more poignant tragedy, one almost worse because it had not yet been fully played out.

CHAPTER
TEN

Sam

After ten years or so in a practice it's a rare and invariably serious matter to be called by someone who's always been on the list but who's still a stranger to you — the alarm bells ring loud.

It had rained almost incessantly through that September, but the first of October dawned fine and bright. I was enjoying the novelty of the morning when the call came in.

"Sorry to bother you, Doctor," came the voice of Mrs McCloy — a cheerful soul in her early thirties whom we saw at intervals, mainly with one or other of her three children — "but I think you'd need to call with Sam Wilson sometime today; he's just been in to ask me to ring you as he's not well, and really" — her voice dropped as voices do when they have something of gravity to impart — "he doesn't look one bit well — he no more than made it to us and Joe had to run him home again in the car."

"Sam Wilson?" I said, not wanting to admit that I didn't know who she was talking about. "Sam Wilson? . . . er . . ."

"Aye, Sam Wilson, Ballymacroarty."

"Ah, well," I thought, "he can't be moribund." If he'd legged it from Ballymacroarty to the McCloys he'd have covered anything from two hundred yards to a mile and a half, depending on just where he lived.

"Remind me now, Mrs McCloy — just whereabouts is Sam's place again? It's a long time since I was last there." (I was sure I'd never been there in my life.)

"Turn down the road just opposite us, go on over the bridge and it's the first lane on the left."

Well, that sounded delightfully straightforward; directions you could trust and understand made life so much easier, I thought, as the car sprayed through the puddles the recent rain had left even on the main road. The low-lying fields alongside were flooded, so much so that I could have done the first part of the trip by canoe just as easily.

Off the main road at McCloy's and down an undulating third class road, round the bend and over the hump back of the old railway bridge. That must be it — a new bungalow a few yards off the road (she'd said it was set back a bit from the road).

I drew up — something wasn't right — children's toys strewn around the garden, a car at the side of the house; hardly what you'd expect of an old man who, as far as I'd understood between the lines of the conversation, lived alone, depending on none-too-close neighbours.

The door was opened by a young woman who recognised me instantly.

"I think I'm at the wrong house," I said by way of introduction.

"You surely are, Doctor, for we're all well here — who is it you're looking?"

"Sam Wilson."

"Ah, now, his place is over there — look, I'll show it to you."

She stepped out of the hallway and we walked to the side of the house: as we did so, the breeze which had blown the rain away slammed the door behind her. A momentary look of consternation crossed her face, but then she smiled and pointed over the undulating wooded ground that lay beyond the fields.

"That's it, that white cottage over there." I could see the chimney and a bit of white gable with a tiny window set high up in it.

"It's the next lane along — you'd need to go slow, now, for you could miss it easy, now."

We were back at the slammed front door. "Oh, dear, I think I've locked myself out." She tried the door: she had.

Now the sensible thing for a busy GP to do at this stage would be to murmur something inconsequential and depart, but I felt some moral obligation here.

"You're sure the back door's locked? Better have a look." It was, too.

I looked around; she shivered — she wasn't dressed for standing around in a freshening autumn wind which, having blown the September rain away, was already whipping up a few darker clouds for the start of the October ration.

"Keys anywhere?"

"No; Colm's away to town for the morning — he'll not be back until two or three o'clock."

"The car key ring — have you a house key on it?"

"In the house," we chorused and began to laugh.

"Better see what we can do, then." I was now well past the point of any departure and I was committed to solving this problem first.

The house was modern with tiny opening sections at the tops of the windows, all designed to deter illicit entry — even had they not been locked shut they would scarcely have allowed my spare frame to squeeze in, let alone this comfortably built lass.

The only window off the latch was the toilet.

"I could try to get in there," I offered, hoping it would sound half-hearted enough to make her think of something else more decorous. Her look meant the offer was accepted with thanks — instantly.

Getting in wasn't all that difficult.

"Doctor, mind the nappies — the place is a bit of a mess yet."

Her warning was too late, but I managed to clear most of them in my head-on slide to the floor, via the toilet pan. The rest was easy, though by now the relief had us both in convulsions of laughter.

At least I now knew where old Sam lived. "God!" I thought suddenly. "I hope he's still alive after all this!" Anyway, come what may, I would need a wash and brush up before going on.

I drove slowly down the road: a field gate, another field gate, then a lane with a bucket full of empty milk bottles at the entrance. This must be it — but the lane was barely ten yards long before ending at a gate to a large pasture in which a few Friesians were quietly passing the day. The cottage lay beyond this almost two hundred yards away and looked quite idyllic at the distance. A quick run along the road confirmed that there was no other laneway, so I backed into the entrance, collected my gear and opened the gate.

Cattle are well known for congregating at the gates of fields, probably out of a desire to see the odd half-dozen vehicles a day go past. Whatever their motive, they had had a great time stamping that bit of field into a quagmire, celebrating their achievement by producing masses of cow pats to mix in with the mud and make the ten yards or so from the gate quite impassable. I hadn't expected this call to be a "walker" — I doubt if we had half a dozen such on the practice then: mind you, there are many places you'd be better walking to, where the "road" is no more than a rough track guaranteed to wreck your shock absorbers and claim a silencer at anything more than five miles an hour; still, they fell within the range of normal for the parish.

The mud made short work of my shoes and socks, even though I edged my way along the hedge to minimise the damage. There was no vestige of a path to be followed, not even a trace of the morning's footprints, so I simply struck out over the grass.

While I was still some distance away, an old man came out from behind the hedge which ran at the back of the house, pulling up his trousers as he did so, and returned to the front door. Obviously, even basic

114

amenities were lacking here, the process of "going to the ground" being still employed; by working one's way from one end of the hedge to the other, you could find the first end "clean" again by the time you got back to it — unless you had a lot of guests or protracted diarrhoea! Still, it ensured wide variety in the hedgerow flora.

He entered the house without noticing me as I came close enough to the garden gate to recognise it as the end of an old iron bedstead, swinging from a wooden post on two loops of fencing wire. It could have looked almost elegant in the right setting, but this wasn't it. The cottage, white-washed, isolated and idyllic from a distance, was crumbling; the rotting windows, protected by scraps of dirty net curtain, looked out on a tiny "garden" — a tangle of weeds and grass separated from the field by a length of chicken wire supported on an assortment of sticks and ready to fall over if any of the cattle so much as breathed on it. From the gate a series of flat stones half-covered in watery mud led to the only door and indeed led on in through it, for it was hard to know just where garden stopped and floor began. I knocked, although as the door was wide open and gave a full view of the room, it seemed hardly necessary.

"Come you on in now," said Sam, rising from an ancient settee in front of the open-hearth fire on which a pile of turf glowed. In its fundamentals the house could have seen little change since the eighteenth century; true, there was an old radio on the dresser and the settee looked nineteen-twenties, but the room belonged to a different age. The doorway offered the main source of light, for the window on the same wall was tiny. In the glow of the turf, rather than the light from the door, I could see the fire crane with its chain and hooks (obviously in daily use, for there was no other apparent way of cooking food) turned aside and the black-encrusted kettle nestled into the glowing turf below it. There was no clock to be seen.

In an armchair to the left of the fire and barely visible in the gloom sat a stout old woman, presumably Mrs Sam. She took no notice of me but nursed a kitten on her lap, crooning to it constantly in a low tuneless way.

In a spot diagnosis I wondered if this was in fact the biggest of Sam's problems — a wife too demented to look after him and he not now well enough to look after her. But no: "Doctor, this past while I've been passing a lot of blood in the water."

"Any pain with it?"

"Ach, well now, there'd be a soreness with it betimes, don't y' know."

"We'd better have a look at you, I think — can we get you lying down somewhere?"

He led the way into the only other room — a bedroom just large enough to hold two double beds with a gap between them, barely wide enough for access.

Sam obviously had a serious problem: my initial conclusion was that he had a carcinoma of his bladder, although apart from the blood, he was having few symptoms. We talked about it for a while and I saw my concern reflected in his face. Further investigation in hospital would be needed. He looked out of the wee bedroom window, his eyes and his thoughts far away. There was a long unspoken conversation between us in those few moments and without a further word being spoken I felt Sam had the situation well weighed up. "Aye, well — whatever you think's best, Doctor; you're the one to know."

(Lord, how often have I heard that said, yet how rarely is it as true as either the patient or the doctor would like to believe!)

To provide what would most content Sam and his wife was not a matter of X-rays or biochemistry; their importance lay more in determining how much longer Sam was going to manage as he was — how long before both of them were toppled from the narrowing tightrope of their lives.

We moved back into the kitchen. The place was swarming with cats who made themselves comfortable around the fire and on the settee; I counted nine before they began moving about and put an end to the census.

Mrs Sam held up the kitten, still in her hands, for my approval: "That's my wee kitty," she said, smiling broadly. I paid it my respects for a few seconds and smiled back at the old woman — sometimes dementia can be a blessing of sorts, hiding the crosses old age brings to those least able to bear them.

I headed back over the field, pondering on the next steps — clearly Sam needed to be investigated and given what help could be given, but what of his wife? Simply to have her uplifted by Social Services and put in a nice clean bed in a nice clean (and cat-free) nursing home would just kill her — and losing her would leave him little zest for clinging on to what was left of life.

Sometimes there are no answers — life's just a real bugger.

CHAPTER ELEVEN

The Spirit of Ulster

The Irishman's relationship with alcohol is the stuff of legend: when the opportunity arises to combine it with cocking a snook at the law, the temptation becomes almost too much to resist.

Ulster is "dry" on Sundays: on this day the public houses are all closed and the church doors flung wide open to welcome the devout of all denominations.

Well, nominally.

Indeed, to the casual visitor that is how it would appear, but in reality things are ordered rather differently. Although to the passer-by an Ulster village on a wet Sunday looks as if it has been wholly abandoned by its population, the locals know better. There are those, not even the most cynical, who would say that, after Saturday, Sunday is the busiest day for some licensed premises. Legend has it that at one establishment a double kick on the bar-room door any time before 3a.m. will ensure that the wicket gate at the side of the building is unlatched when the kicker returns two minutes later; regulars at other places all know the code for entry to their favoured haunt.

One place, a nondescript wee hole-in-the-wall, little different from any of its fellows in the town (or even in the whole country), was run by a duo of ageing spinsters who ruled a slightly younger bachelor brother in much the same way as they ran the pub: "No nonsense, no gross drunkenness, no bad language and no bad behaviour, or you get out and don't come back!" The customers, large, belligerent and rowdy as many might have been at other times, became as sheep before their octogenarian hostesses and did as they were told — always.

My visits were almost always to the brother, well on in his seventies and with reasonably controlled cardiac failure. They always began with a panic-stricken phone call, but the first priority on arrival was never the patient, but the proffering of a large glass of brandy. Once, in a moment of weakness, the sort that come on when confronted by a well-stocked bar and the insistent offer of a drink, I'd agreed to take "a wee spot of brandy", although I didn't really want it and wouldn't normally drink on duty anyway. On that occasion the "wee drop" came out at about a quarter of a pint and having then seen the brother and taken my leave, I reeled out into the road as it came up to meet me and drove home hoping that the constabulary was engaged elsewhere. Ever after that, without a word being spoken, a huge glass of brandy greeted my arrival; I could well have done without it, but at least it sweetened the bitter pill of a late-night call to a problem that should have been dealt with at a more appropriate time.

120

One such Sunday I was ushered, via the usual brandy, into the back kitchen to give Brother his once-over — there wasn't much fresh to find, but I wasn't in any great hurry and passed a few minutes chatting with the sisters at the end of the examination. Then there came a soft tap on the door which led from the kitchen to the hallway of the public part of the house. This was a little odd, for all the family were in the room with me and until then the house had been utterly silent.

A fleeting glance of concern passed between the sisters, then as we continued chatting, one rose and casually went to the door, opening it only far enough to let herself through sideways. Had she been a wee wisp of a woman I might have seen nothing but she had to open the door fairly far to slip through, even sideways, and I glanced across the room to the hall, in pitch darkness as the Sunday shutters were up.

It was packed with people: a sea of faces, indistinguishable in the gloom, moved round in silent shuffling to let mine hostess in and the door closed behind her.

I realised that not only had I stopped in mid sentence but in the second or two it took for all this, I'd forgotten what I'd been saying and was sitting with some syllable or other waiting to fall from my open, too-open mouth.

I smiled gently, a "Yes-I-know-all-about-it-but-I'm-not-going-to-say-anything" smile, and the conversation was picked up as we'd left it, although there was a hint of relief in the tone of the chat. I left eventually on our

121

usual very friendly terms, allowing myself only a gentle wink at the senior sister as she showed me out. Her mischievous grin in response took about thirty years off her for an instant and I saw beyond her ageing form to someone who, I bet, was quite a girl in her time.

Strange, though, I was never called back there on a Sunday after that. Probably just as well — I'm sure I'm better off without the brandy and besides, "I never drink when I'm on duty."

Legal spirits, even out of hours, are one thing; poteen, the home-distilled spirit made often in surprisingly large quantities without the blessing of the Customs and Excise Department, is quite another. Added to the skill of making stuff that's good enough to sell is the thrill of the chase and the challenge of staying at least one step ahead of Authority.

I had, one bad day, two victims of fatal poisoning from a bad batch of poteen; I suspect that whoever made it had neglected to throw away the fluid that comes over first. This is by tradition always given to the fairies — the fact that it consists very largely of the highly toxic methyl alcohol (turns you blind, mad and dead in fairly quick succession) I have always blamed for the fact that there are no fairies left in Ireland now — well, not of that sort, anyway.

Any maker worth the name will turn out perfectly good liquor — after all, it's bad for trade if your customers snuff it after an evening on the stuff — but within the ranks of the regiment of makers there is always a hierarchy of quality.

One afternoon I took a call from a GP based about ten or twelve miles away. "I've just been out to a man I haven't seen for years — in fact, I thought he must have died and I'd missed the event. He's lying in an outhouse of an old farm that's used for a hay store. No one has any idea of how long he's been there, but it can't have been all that long or he'd be dead by now. It looks as if he's got an advanced malignancy somewhere, probably bowel; you'll not be fit to do much for him but he needs to be in with you. As far as I know, he has no one to call on as next-of-kin — always a loner, y'know."

In due course, Big John wheeled in on the ambulance trolley a filthy bundle of rags containing an emaciated body. "I don't think he'll be with us much longer, God help him," said John. "Would you ever look at the state of him, and him well-enough off, by all accounts."

"Really? Hard to believe now, looking at him," I said as we rolled him, too far gone to groan, onto the bed. Such of a story as I could obtain, and the basic physical examination, bore out the opinions of both doctor and driver. We set about making him comfortable and rehydrating him, for his spell in the outhouse had made him even worse than he should have been. He made some response to this, at least to the extent of being able to give us a history, although it didn't add much to what we'd already gleaned.

He hadn't been in more than a few hours when the visitors began to arrive, a steady stream of middle-aged men, all seemingly keen to have a confidential conversation with him. Some stayed only a few moments, some stayed a lot longer — for a man found as he had been, he was being remarkably assiduously visited.

I got my answer when his GP called to see another of his patients.

"How's Johnny — is he still with us?" he asked me.

"Oh, yes, in fact for a man as neglected as that he's having a whole army of visitors — it's amazing".

"Ah, well, there's a reason for that, y'see: there lies the best poteen maker in the Six Counties — and half the countryside's looking the recipe, wanting to know his secrets before he takes them beyond recall."

"D'ye think he'll give them out?"

"Not him! Even if he knows he's going, he'll take them with him just to spite them all!"

And for all I know, he did. Not that you can ask anyone, of course!

Liquor, both legal and occasionally otherwise, was in those days the stable currency of gratitude to professionals: many a medical and legal drinks cabinet survived from one Christmas to another on donations from patients and clients.

Sean was a fairly regular attender, mainly because he was eighty-odd and gathering the problems of being eighty-odd. But he was always cheerful and consultations with him were a pleasure, the session always enlivened with a bit of entertaining craic. Once he'd discovered that we weren't teetotal he always brought in a bottle or two of his home brew. Home-brewed beer

124

varies from the ghastly to the excellent and as Sean's was closer to the latter than the former, it was always gratefully received.

At the end of one consultation he said with a conspiratorial wink, "I'll leave you a bottle of some special stuff by the car, Doctor — your man'll enjoy it even if it's not to your taste."

"Thanks very much; I'll look out for it."

In fact, I'd almost forgotten it by the end of the surgery and was working through the lists of repeat prescriptions when Joanne, our practice nurse, came flying into the reception area which served as nerve centre, waiting room watchtower and, at this moment, office. She was as white as a sheet, her eyes wide open, staring. "Doctor, doctor," she exclaimed, "it's awful . . . there's . . . there's . . . *something* under your car — it's just by the wheel — I think it could be a bomb — we need to ring the police."

(At this time, this wasn't such a silly idea as it might seem — the booby-trap bomb was just beginning to wreak its own horrible brand of devastation in the province, so she wasn't entirely crazy.)

"No, don't bother," I said — well, she was always a nervous creature and I couldn't resist running this one a bit longer. "I'll just kick it out of the way then we can ring the bomb disposal people."

Before her panic-stricken gaze and in spite of her begging me not to go near it, I went into the car park. Sure enough, there was Sean's parcel, roughly tied up in his own identifiable style, planted neatly behind the front wheel. He'd obviously had more faith in my memory than was justified, for I could so easily have forgotten, hopped into the car and smashed it before remembering. Still, there it was and as Joanne, and one or two others drawn by the commotion, watched horrified, I picked up the parcel and popped it on the front seat. The reaction to this was such that I felt it was time to come clean, before I found myself with multiple resuscitations on my hands.

"It's OK, it's just a bottle or two of home brew that Sean left this morning — he said he'd put it here."

Attitudes changed: relief first, then, "You knew all along — you could have said — I've never been so scared in all my life — you could have told us!"

"Sorry, but I couldn't resist it, seeing your face — it was a treat!"

It was days before I was really forgiven for that.

When I brought it home and opened it after telling the story, we found, not home brew, but a bottle of fine poteen. Hugh's only comment was, "It'd have been a tragedy if you'd run over that — it's damn good stuff — in fact it's even better than the bottle I got last month from that policeman."

Funny old country, Ireland.

CHAPTER
TWELVE

The Hut

"Doctor, I wonder could you call out and see my father? He's having a lot of trouble with his water."

The voice was youngish, female and personable, but the name and address were unknown to me and the directions were such that even as I left home I hadn't quite got a visual idea of where he lived. The fact that it was eleven o'clock on a late October night wasn't going to help: the area was one where at that time people didn't answer night-time knocks at the door unless they were expecting you and my chances of getting further directions would be slim enough.

However, I found what seemed to be the laneway at the first go. She had said, "Go to the second bungalow and it's just beside that" — though what "it" was wasn't specified.

The headlights showed a broad rough laneway, but little else — the blackness beyond the light beam was absolute. The lights picked out a roadside bungalow. "That's one," I thought, and sure enough a few dozen yards later a second one reflected a few stray beams from the lights. As instructed, I turned in between it and a shadow, just a shade darker than the surrounding blackness, which I assumed was an outhouse. I stopped the engine and switched off the lights. I was in total blackness, so much so that I was afraid to leave the car in case I couldn't find it again. Even as my eyes grew accustomed to the darkness, I could make out nothing — there was certainly no light pollution here (although I don't think the phrase had come into the language then), and I had not made things easier for myself by forgetting to check before setting off that the torch which lived in the car was in fact there — it wasn't.

I went to the bungalow and groped round for the bell, having first groped round for the front steps, then for the door. Eventually I gave up looking for the bell, but managed to find a knocker, which I put to good use. There was a response, but not from the bungalow — instead a door opened in the black mass across the way, letting out a chink of dim light; by the standards of the blackness around, it seemed like sunrise.

"Doctor?" came the query, the voice that of my caller.

"Yes, it's me," I said, groping my way back down the steps and homing in on the light.

I realised as I entered that the black mass was in fact a large Nissen hut; inside, it had most of the trappings of habitability — a living room with a fire, whose red glow had been my source of light as the door opened, with a settee and a couple of armchairs, all of which had seen better days.

"He's in the bedroom," said my informant, a charming and attractive, not-quite-forty lass. "He's been off colour for a few days and having a lot of pain trying to pass water."

He lay on the old bed, a spare wiry man, looking maybe in his early seventies. This at least I could see; he had a pressure lantern which provided light, warmth, condensation and a steady background hiss to our conversation.

The initial impression of prostate trouble began to wear a bit thin as the history unfolded; bits were just not right and despite the circumstances I was going to have to examine him in detail. There was nothing remarkable until I came to the rectal examination, when my finger ran up against a stony hard mass projecting backwards — very suspicious of a malignancy in the prostate.

"Look, I can't do very much more tonight," I said. "We need to get you down to the hospital clinic and see just what's going on here. I'll sort this out for you in the morning, if that's all right with you."

"Aye, surely, Doctor — you'd be the one to know, now," came the reply. No questioning of the need and no need of confirmation of the seriousness of the situation — that was all unspoken and understood.

I spoke to the Duty Surgeon the next morning and told him the story.

"I could see him at the end of tomorrow's clinic," he said after checking his list. (What would one not give for that sort of service today, but this "wasn't today nor yesterday", as they say here.) This was duly arranged and I let more pressing matters take precedence in my thoughts.

The surgeon caught up with me the next day. "That's an interesting old boy you sent me," he said. "The one you thought was a malignant prostate."

"'What I thought was . . .'?" I repeated, aware that I was about to be proved wrong. "What did you think of it then?"

"I reckon he's got the biggest bladder stone I've ever felt; it's just too hard to be anything else. I'm getting him investigated as a matter of urgency. We should get him slotted in next week, but I'll keep you informed."

I went off, rehearsing again the physical feel of a bladder stone, something I'd never come across before. They used to be fairly common a few centuries ago and provided work for surgeons and itinerant "Cutters for the Stone", people whose reputation depended on their survival rates, rates which were often better than those of the "Regular" surgeons. In western society at least they had become a bit of a rarity and it was interesting to come across one in the practice. I made a mental note to check with X-ray when he was booked to come down; I could at least call in on him — he'd never been in hospital before and the sight of one face he'd actually met before might be some reassurance to him — besides, I'd be able to see the films as they fell from the processor.

Fate decreed differently, however: I met the surgeon in the corridor early the following week. Again he stopped me.

"Your man with the bladder calculus won't be keeping his appointment — I've just had a call from his daughter. She found him dead in bed this morning."

130

CHAPTER
THIRTEEN

Alarm Bells

To be fair to our patients they were, almost to a family, considerate of our nights. Even the most demanding, who'd think nothing of ringing in at nine or ten o'clock of an evening, tended to soldier on during the wee small hours, keeping their symptoms often into the middle of the next morning. So when you get a call at two in the morning from someone you don't know, a multitude of alarm bells ring.

"Doctor, could you come out to Twenty, Queen's Park? It's Janet: she's gone mad!"

The call was made all the more urgent by a background sound of a woman screaming what sounded like abuse — anyway, it didn't sound like something to procrastinate over.

The house was one of an old terrace of brick cottages (I imagine the eponymous Queen was Victoria), most of them owner-occupied, although they had originally been cottages tied to the Big Mill which dominated that part of the small town. Number 20 was easily found; it was the only one with all the lights on and I was hardly out of the car before it defined itself further by the sounds of high-pitched shouting and screaming. I'm quite sure all the neighbours had been woken by it but were too polite to draw attention to the fact by putting their own lights on and betraying their curiosity. The door was ajar and I went in without knocking, following the sound through to the back kitchen.

Janet, an attractive-looking woman of about thirty, was standing wild-eyed and staring, facing her parents. By the look of them, none of them had been to bed and I wondered how long this had been going on before they'd rung me. The situation wasn't helped by the fact that she was brandishing the family carving knife with vigour but little sense of purpose or direction. Sense of purpose or not, disarming her by force was not an option. I tugged at her mother's sleeve and drew her away from the front line.

"What on earth's happened here?" My question conveyed some of my own sense of surprise because, frankly, Janet just didn't look the type to be behaving like this. (It was long before the days of widespread illicit drug addiction — I doubt if there was even one "hard drug" user on the practice at that time and we certainly didn't know of any.) She was well-dressed, well-groomed; the house and her parents neat and tidy: and the observed behaviour didn't fit with anything save perhaps an acute psychosis coming right out of the blue.

"Doctor, she's not been herself for a good wee while, now — she's been very moody and seems to be badly failed; I've been trying to get her to come and see you but she wouldn't, and what with her working away during the week I just don't know what's been going on. Even when she's here, she hardly seems to sleep, for I can hear her wrecking around at all hours o' the night — but she's never been like this before."

Not quite the picture of a psychosis out of the blue, then. As I watched and listened from the passageway outside the kitchen, I felt that what I was witnessing was not primarily psychiatric — there was some logic, however distorted, in her tirade. I gathered up my courage and approached her, speaking quietly and being as restrained as I could be. The result was almost immediate and dramatic; she stopped her flow of words, threw down the knife and burst into floods of tears, becoming even less comprehensible as she tried to go on talking through the sobs. Meanwhile I was looking at her with an ever-growing interest and clinical fascination: she was indeed painfully thin, her well-tailored clothes (she was working in the city and doing all right for herself, according to her mother) almost hanging off her, but what impressed me most were her eyes: even when downcast as she sobbed, her eyes were still staring — but it wasn't a stare, once I had a proper look; it was protruberance, the lids drawn back to expose the whites above the blue centres. The alarm bells at the beginning of the call were ringing again, but this time in a carillon.

A look at her neck showed the now-expected thyroid gland swelling: the rapid pulse and the tremor of her hands almost completed the classical diagnosis of an acute thyrotoxicosis. I spent a few seconds savouring the sweet heady vapour of success, until I was interrupted by the anxious voice of her mother, who drew me aside, away from the room and back into the passageway.

"Doctor, will she . . . will she have to . . . have to be . . . put away, d'ye think?" Mental illness still carried a sense of shame and stigmatisation then — things are a lot better now, but even so, shades of it persist. At that time, if you had had an episode of psychiatric illness, the neighbours didn't ask how you were; they just discussed it when you'd left.

"No, but she's going to have to go into hospital tonight, for she needs urgent treatment — but if all goes well, as I expect it will, you'll see a big change on her in the next week or so and she'll be back to her old self in a few months."

There's always an awful lot of pleasure in being able to say something like that to an anxious patient or relative — saying it while being secretly smug at picking up an oddity in the middle of the night only adds to the pleasure, but I kept the smugness for the ears of the admitting doctor when I phoned him a few minutes later. He sounded impressed, but that could just have been his way of getting me off the phone sooner.

CHAPTER
FOURTEEN

The Witches' Cottage

Most houses were known to us, not by the number in the street, but as "Johnny, the prostate on the Burn Drive at the bend" or "Bernadette, the ovarian cyst at [whatever townland it was]". Designation by first name and pathology alone could have been enough for most occasions, but there was one exception where we never seemed to be able to bring to mind the name, but the nickname we had for the house was all that was necessary: to say "The Witches' Cottage" conveyed all we needed to know.

It had, I think, originally been built as the gatehouse to what was once the largest estate in the area, although as time went on big houses and big estates found it harder to hold themselves together. The Big House gradually fell into decay, the loss of the heir to the place in the Second World War (so we heard) putting the seal on its fate.

The lodge survived, it and its bit of ground (in fact an acre or two of woodland which very effectively screened it from the road) taking on an independent existence long after the Big House had been demolished and the ruins hidden under a nondescript

135

housing estate. The striking thing was the style in which
it was built: eschewing both the vernacular and the
neo-classical, either of which could have sat comfortably with the style of the Big House, the house had a
black-and-white half-timbered construction which
might have looked fine in Kent or Sussex but stuck out
like the proverbial sore thumb in rural Ulster. It was
perhaps as well that the woodland screened it so well; it
could sit there without drawing attention to itself.

I'd been in the practice a few months before I even
learned of the existence of the place, when the
receptionist, reeling off the list of calls for the day, said,
"Old Mrs Mc . . . at the Witches' Cottage." She saw
from my open mouth and startled expression that this
was a new one to me and filled me in on such details as
she knew of the place, for the loss of the Big House and
the associated changes had all been before her time in
the town. She excused my ignorance of the place with,
"Well, I suppose they *have* been quiet for a while."
There was something ominous in her tone, but I didn't
follow it up.

It wasn't very far to go and was on my way home, so
the visit was left till last before lunch. I'd been primed
on where to find the entrance into the wood — and it
was just as well I had been, for the hole in the hedge
looked just like an entry into a forest footpath, rather
than the driveway to a private house.

With its collection of steeply sloping roofs at
different heights and odd angles to each other, its tall
narrow brick chimneys and an abundance of small
latticed windows, it reminded me of childhood pictures

of the Gingerbread House in "Hansel and Gretel": you could see how it had come by its nickname. Getting out of the car, I wondered if I'd leave as a little gingerbread doctor, complete with currants for waistcoat buttons and a little gingerbread oblong for a bag. The musing stopped very suddenly as the door was opened with a promptness so startling that I reckoned she'd had her hand on the latch, just awaiting my knock out of politeness.

Still indistinct in the gloom of the interior was an old crone, slightly stooped, her mouth split into what I took for a welcoming smile.

"Ah, Doctor," she said, eying me up and down (suddenly the idea of the gingerbread didn't seem so remote after all). "Come on in — you're the new man, aren't you?"

She appeared to have most of her teeth and there was no sign of broomstick, pointed hat or black cat, so in I went. In fact the place was so dark that I could see very little at all at first. As I adapted to it, I saw a small living room filled to overflowing with an assortment of things that most families leave out for the binman every week. Cardboard boxes from the shops, newspapers by the hundredweight, piles of clothes of indeterminate age and state, sticks and logs strewn beside the fire, gas cylinders (too close to the fire for my peace of mind) — so much stuff that it was a while before I recognised the three or four old stuffed chairs and the table with a pile of unwashed dishes and the heel of a loaf on it.

All this I took in in a second or two, trying not to move my head; after all, it doesn't do to appear too

137

curious about other people's possessions. I smiled back and said, "Well now, what seems to be the trouble? You don't look too bad to me." (I was young then — I have long since dropped this line as an opener, for it invariably gives the recipient full rein to explain at inordinate length that they *are* too bad.)

"Oh, I'm middling meself — it's me mother I called you to see."

Her mother? Her *mother*? She has a mother, *alive*? Some furious mental arithmetic reassured me that even her mother would have escaped being burned or ducked to death, if only just.

"She must be a brave age now, your mother," I blurted out tactlessly and rather more loudly than was necessary, as I made to sit down on the nearest of the chairs, which like its fellows, was half-filled with old clothes.

"I'll be ninety-seven next April," came an edentulous cackle from just below my backside — one of the bundles of clothing had spoken as I was on the point of lowering myself onto it. The surprise and the sudden reversal of direction caused my thigh muscles to ache for a day afterwards: it's also difficult to pretend you were going to do something quite different, but at least they had the good grace to seem to ignore it. I put on the best show I could, steering myself round to face the chair and its bundle, taking a bit more notice of it this time. Right enough, somewhere near the top of the bundle was a tiny wrinkled face, framed in strands of grey hair which merged into the darker grey of what I now saw as a shawl; it in turn blended with the rest of the old clothing on the chair back. In the prevailing gloom it was little wonder that I'd missed an occupant — as it was, it was hard to make out where she began and ended. The wrinkles deepened into a smile, giving me a landmark as well as a welcome.

"It's her chist, Doctor," said the Young Witch. "She does always be troubled with it at this time o' year." I looked at the pitifully small fire — a few lumps of half-consumed turf contributing little that was positive to the room — and at the ancient wallpaper, darkened with damp and peeling off the wall by the yard; add to this the gutters which seemed incapable of directing water anywhere but down the walls in a steady overflowing dribble, enough to be a conspicuous feature at first glance on arrival, and I could see ample reason why she would be troubled with her chist. Still, it seemed to have served her well enough for the best part of a century and, as one of my old tutors used to maintain, "You can't argue with success." Yes, the old place could be almost idyllic in a long hot dry summer, but you don't get many of those in Ulster; usually all that happens is that the summer rain is a bit warmer.

I was going to have to examine her chest. Now, at medical school one is taught the routine of chest examination: "Inspection (look at it), Palpation (feel it), Percussion (knock on it), Auscultation (listen to it)." All of this is practised on nice clean co-operative patients sitting to attention in their nice clean hospital beds. I often think of those days and wonder if those who so strictly hammered the routine into us really believed that all patients are like that, out in the real world. They told us nothing about how to draw valid conclusions from an immobile bundle of clothing many layers thick when even the section called "Inspection" is a non-starter.

The upper clothing rose and fell ever so slightly so I settled for that as the Inspection section — she was breathing. I had already decided to skip the intermediate stages. "I need to listen to your chest a wee minute," I bawled into her ear, forgetting that she'd already heard less noise at greater range.

"It's all right, Doctor, dear; I'm not deaf, just getting a bit hard of hearing now, but the years is there and you can't do anything about that, now." She grinned; I was beginning to take to the old girl.

We tussled for a few minutes, the Young Witch, the Old Dear and myself, hindering as much as helping each other, but finally succeeded in exposing about six square inches of upper chest (mainly the bony bits), from which all deductions would have to be made and acted upon. I wriggled the end of a stethoscope down the back of her now-loosened clothing, hoping that it was inside and not on top of the last vest and praying that the shades of my tutors were directing their attentions somewhere else.

Aha! Basal crepitations! I listened for a while to be sure it wasn't just a vest moving, but it was plain enough, sounding more like fluid at the lung bases than infection pure and simple. Her pulse had been almost too faint to assess, but I could hear the heart sounds well enough by the time I'd moved the stethoscope as far round to the front as I could. Aha! — irregularly irregular and quite fast. The picture was piecing itself together now. The next step was to look for swelling of the ankles; usually this is done so quickly that it hardly needs mention, but here again there was a barrier to penetrate. I got down on the floor almost like a Muslim at prayer and began to tackle her lower extremities. First the encompassing blanket was hauled out of the way to reveal a set of gaiters made from layers of newspapers rolled around the leg; next came the stockings — by the time I'd reached the third layer of these I was beginning to wonder if it was worth going on, but under them lay skin: never mind that it hadn't seen daylight for — well, God knows how long; it was skin nonetheless. And, yes, it was worthwhile; the ankles and lower parts of the legs were swollen with oedema. Despite appearances, I gathered that she was reasonably mobile during the day, so the swelling was more likely to be coming from a degree of heart failure.

I was now well enough used to the gloom to see that under the grime the Old Dear was as white as a sheet, indeed a good bit whiter than the sheets in the room: she was grossly anaemic. Maybe I could simply have given her some iron and something to reduce the fluid build-up, but "in for a penny, in for a pound" was taking over and I felt duty-bound to investigate the anaemia. This meant taking blood and if getting a stethoscope down her back was awkward, it was nothing to exposing an elbow, finding a vein and putting a needle into it; this was where the hard apprenticeship of years of setting up drips on collapsed patients in the middle of the night by the miserable light of a bedside locker lamp, with only a terrified very junior nurse for help, came into its own, and the job was done reasonably easily once access had been gained.

My patient was visibly impressed. "Eh, eh, Doctor," she cackled, "no one's ever done that to me before!"

I bet they hadn't.

The blood test revealed an iron-deficiency anaemia (like so many in their situation, they lived on bread and tea). We didn't push investigations any further and she did well on the iron, almost making her century before pneumonia, the friend of all the old and tired in the world, quietly took her away with scarcely a murmur of protest.

CHAPTER
FIFTEEN

Brushes with the Law

Everyone in medicine sooner or later come in contact with the workings of the law, although unless they're very foolish or very unlucky they'll be in the witness box and not the dock. Their opinions will be listened to in silence and with obvious respect, while they waffle on — I mean, offer the court the benefit of their years of accumulated knowledge and wisdom in assisting it to reach a fair and meaningful conclusion to the case in hand . . .. Mmmmmm.

At the time of my first foray into this alien world, my years of experience could be numbered on the fingers, indeed the thumb, of one hand; still, I had a medical degree, which no one else in the room had, something which gives you a good hand in the Confidence Game. Not that this initiation was any big deal — not for me the high-profile court action with the ranks of the press hanging onto and writing down your every word as you get your fifteen minutes of fame; this baptism was on an early spring morning in a nearby village in a courthouse (now long, long closed) to which I'd been summoned to provide evidence of injuries sustained in an alleged assault, the end result of a Saturday night disagreement a week or so previously.

The courthouse, which from the outside looked quite elegant in a provincial neo-classical way, failed dismally to live up to its exterior once you went inside. The furnishings, all made from tongue-groove-and-bead pine, subordinated aesthetics (and just about everything else) to functionality; the style, such as it was, came straight from the latter half of the nineteenth century and so, I reckoned, did its last coat of paint, applied at a time when chocolate and dirty cream were not only fashionable but in abundant supply. The windows, set high in the walls, deterred not only potential escapers but potential window-cleaners — and showed it.

The congregation, a shifty-looking, ill-dressed bunch already gathered on the hard chocolate-coloured benches, seemed to fit perfectly into this time-warp: sitting in clutches on either side of the central aisle like the Bride's Side and the Groom's Side at a wedding, they chatted among themselves in small groups while waiting for proceedings to start. The room was presided over by a single RUC sergeant who kept a low profile at the back of the room, warming himself by the pot-bellied stove there, for there was a nip in the air and the stove was all the heating there was; as sergeant, he was going to have his share of it first. I made my way over to him and introduced myself.

"Ah, that's fine: just find a seat somewhere — we'll get ye out as soon as we can. RM's not turned up yet." Old terms die hard, and the sitting magistrate still unofficially carried the soubriquet of Resident Magistrate, always abbreviated to RM, a term made immortal by Somerville and Ross in their early twentieth century book, *Reminiscences of an Irish RM* — compulsory reading for anyone who ever contemplates living in Ireland, even if it was written almost a century ago. But I knew that the modern justice system wouldn't tolerate such shenanigans as they had described.

The door behind the bench opened and the RM entered, or rather, shambled in, nodded to the assembled standing company, undid the belt of a mackintosh which had certainly seen far better days and, keeping it on, sat down, polishing his spectacles as, without further ceremony, he called the first case. The sergeant moved from his place of warmth and took up his other role, that of Prosecution witness. (Considering he was the only one there in uniform and had all these duties to perform, it looked as if he was in for a busy time of it.)

The first case, the first of many such, was "riding a bicycle without lights". In rural Ulster at that time this was hardly a hanging matter; indeed, the surprise was that he'd been picked up at all, and it was disposed of in about a minute, the defendant leaving the court all of five shillings poorer for his sins. After an hour's worth of this sort of thing, punctuated by the odd constable sidling in to give evidence, then sidling out again, even a first-timer like me was beginning to feel the tedium: what the RM must have felt I could only guess, though I wouldn't have minded betting that behind the glasses the eyes were quite glazed over after the first two or three cases.

Eventually matters moved on to my case. At last there was some animation from the Bench, the Sergeant and, especially, the congregation, most of which last, it seemed, had some concern with the affair. The charge was read out to a stocky little man who'd come up into the dock from the Groom's Side of the aisle.

"I did nothing of the sort, yer honour!" (Even the old courtesy titles were still current, it seemed.)

"I take it that's a 'Not Guilty', then," said the RM.

"That's a damned lie!" came from a very similar-looking figure on the Bride's Side.

"The only liar in this place is you, I swear to God!"

"Silence in court!" called the RM — but the constraints which had kept the rival parties to the case (for such they all were) silent and separated so far were gone in seconds and the match had been put to the powder. In what seemed no time at all, at least half a dozen from each camp were on their feet and setting about their opposite numbers — at first verbally, but very quickly physically. I watched from my seat, glad that I'd chosen to sit at the back, for as well as being out of the way I had a great view of the proceedings. The poor sergeant was hopelessly outnumbered, although at one point I noticed him fingering his revolver holster with a longing look on his face as he tried to restore order by less drastic means.

My eye caught the RM and the image remains with me yet. It was not that he was banging his gavel and calling for order — that was to be expected; what struck me was the attitude — weary, thoroughly brassed-off,

146

had-it-up-to-the-back-teeth-so-many-times despair, as he hammered away on the bench, knowing that he was wasting his time and that lunch would be late again.

Eventually, I know not how — probably they just got tired of the affray — some order was restored and I gave my evidence, in a more respectful silence than I could ever have expected a few short minutes before. The case was concluded in no time at all after that (I can't remember what penalties were laid down, but I assume all parties were bound over to keep the peace).

I stopped by the sergeant as I made my way out. "Is it always like this?" I asked.

"Sure, I told them we'd need two or three of us in here when that lot's in court," he said. "Those two families have been at each other since before I was born an' they're not going to change now, whatever you do with them. Here, ye'd better let me sign your claim form, or ye'll get no expenses."

The form duly signed, I went outside. The narrow village street was full of cars and lorries making their way through the bottleneck in a thoroughly mid-twentieth-century manner. But behind the courthouse doors, I knew that the spirits of Somerville and Ross were alive and well.

The other sort of court to which junior doctors get invited is the coroner's court, when they have been involved in certifying death in circumstances which warrant investigation. The commonest of these to us was the road traffic accident, when usually all we had to do was to present a prepared statement giving an outline of the story of the event as far as we knew it at first hand, together with a note of any injuries seen on external examination: formal postmortem reports were strictly the province of the appointed pathologist and the most we might be asked to do would have been to read out and explain any technicalities in the report — pathologists themselves were almost never called to give evidence in person. The whole business was, and still is, investigative and rarely adversarial, a philosophy which allows a much less formal atmosphere than you'd find in the criminal or civil divisions of the system.

Our Coroner at the time was one of a dying breed even then, a local GP who had come into the post years before I knew him. A real gentleman, he had the GP's skill at putting people at their ease; in court, in the often-tragic circumstances of an inquest, this was an invaluable asset. This gentle informality probably was taken a bit further than the Legal Eagles might have smiled on, but the end result was as good as, perhaps even in some ways better than, a more strict, "by the book" approach might have attained.

His sitting began in the afternoon, when his morning surgery and the day's visits were over. By then, the farming community had most of its essential tasks done and could make it to court with no more trouble than a trip to market — an arrangement which suited everyone. Jurors were not hard to find; in fact, many of them were regulars — retired policemen or others who had had some connection with the legal process and at least knew how the system worked. One in particular had been jury foreman for the past decade or so and could have run an inquest himself, had he been allowed to.

I strolled down through the town in the warmth of a June afternoon and entered the courthouse, only marginally more user-friendly than the scene of my debut, but warmed literally and psychologically by the shafts of sunlight coming in from the same sort of high-set windows. I found a seat near the jury box, exchanging nods with one or two of the jurors whom I'd met as patients. One of them, who lived not far from me, pulled out a pouch of tobacco and lit up his pipe after offering me a bowlful, an offer which I accepted, although until then it wouldn't have occurred to me to smoke in court. We exchanged a few words between puffs and were joined by the Man himself, who also took up the offer of a fill.

"We've four on today," said the coroner; "You'll do foreman as usual, I take it?"

Acquiescence was by a murmur and a minute nod — he'd have been amazed not to have been asked and refusal was just as unthinkable. Three wisps of smoke coiled contemplatively upwards.

". . . this one I'll take first, for the deceased's sister needs to get back to lift the weans from school an' we'll let her away soon as we can, eh?"

"Aye, aye . . ." A curl of blue smoke rose. ". . . awfu' sad business, that . . . and him so young, eh?"

"Aye . . . anyway, there's no doubt about that one; that's a 'Natural Causes' — post-mortem report's quite clear, so it won't take more than a few minutes."

"Now this next one's a bit more of a problem . . . tragic, tragic business, but I reckon there'll be questions asked — I see Jimmy McNulty's here, representing the family, I imagine."

The foreman grinned. "He'll be good for twenty minutes at least . . . anyway, I think he's a way-out relative of the wife — I mean the widow — isn't he?"

"Could be . . . anyway, I think it has to be an 'Accidental Death' . . . I don't think we'll go for 'Misadventure' here, although there'll be a civil case out of it, that's for sure."

Not for the first time in my still-brief career, I was beginning to feel quite redundant, a spurious authority-figure who would have minimal effect on the proceedings of the afternoon: the real work was done under the curling plumes of pipe smoke long before the court went into session.

"This next one's yours, Doctor, isn't it? When you've given your evidence, would you mind hanging on in the witness box for a while, for I'll ask you to read out the post-mortem report and maybe explain to the jury the technical terms if they ask — would you mind?"

At last, I was going to be useful! The thought was tempered by the realisation that the coroner himself was probably more capable than I was of providing all the translation needed, but felt, quite properly, that it would be better coming from a different source.

The fourth case was similarly dealt with:

". . . and you'll mind to express the condolences of the court to the bereaved, now, won't you?"

150

"Oh, aye . . . surely," said the foreman, the smile betraying the regularity of the request. In many other circumstances this could have been a mere empty form of words, but I knew that in this close community where all were known to each other, even if only indirectly, condolences from the jury would come from the heart, not just the lips. "No man is an island . . ."

After all that the hearings themselves were quiet and unhurried; the business was conducted with a kindliness, warmth and sense of personal involvement in the tragedies being retold, almost as if they were being recited to newly arrived friends at a wake, rather than in a Court of Law.

The cases completed (I'd stayed on until the end out of interest, having been involved, so to speak, from the beginning), I left the courthouse feeling oddly uplifted by it all. Even if the procedure had been a touch unorthodox, the formalities had all been accomplished with justice and the minimum of disturbance to those most affected: many a one could learn from an afternoon like that.

In general, junior doctors didn't become involved in the workings of the higher Courts, the Assizes (now the Crown court) for criminal and the County or High courts for civil cases. Unless you had an indispensable role to play, these loftier institutions were the preserve of the more experienced, usually specialist, practitioners, able to hold their own on cross-examination and put forward a cogent case in a comprehensible form.

In the nature of the business, most of our involvement with the criminal courts was for Grievous Bodily Harm in all its aspects, flavoured only rarely with a murder or anything more intellectually taxing to the medical witness.

A distant court and a criminal hearing of a charge of GBH offered me a day out in another part of the province; indeed, just getting there and back would take a few hours and I wasn't going to meet anyone I knew whom I could pass the time with — except the victim, and he was going to be otherwise occupied, even if he remembered me.

So it was with relief and some pleasure that I discovered that the other medical witness was one of my old junior colleagues, who'd taken up practice in the area a few years earlier. Time passed while we caught up on each other's doings, but inevitably the conversation came around to the matter in hand — a locally prominent businessman stood accused of "Causing Grievous Bodily Harm". On the face of it, things looked black for him; I ventured this opinion, to be told, "Oh, he'll be acquitted, no doubt of it."

"What makes you so sure?" I asked.

"As I was coming in to the courthouse, I met half a dozen of my patients, all women, coming in. I said, 'What are you all doing here — coming to sit down between shops, eh?'

"'Oh no,' says one of them; 'We're on the jury today — we've come to get Mr . . . off!' So you see, an acquittal is a near-certainty."

"Not much point in being here at all then," I said.

"Oh, I dunno — it's better than working!"

I could only think of a passage in an old book about the doings at one of the Circuit Courts in the far west of Ireland in the late nineteenth century; after an unwarranted acquittal, the judge's only comment to the accused was, "You have been acquitted by a Limerick jury and you may leave the court with no other stain on your character."

Limerick may have changed, but the philosophy lives on.

It may be an achievement of sorts to get an undeserved acquittal; to cause a trial to be abandoned in chaos demands a different order of skill or, more likely, low cunning.

Every village has its "wino", just as it had (or has) its idiot. Towns have a few, while in the cities they abound in droves.

Jimmy, our most conspicuous one, divided his time between the main street, the Courthouse and the local prison. Visits to the two last usually came towards the end of the year, for it had become almost an ambition of his to ensure that his Christmases were spent "inside" (it says a great deal for the quality of his home life when Christmas in the Nick is the indisputably better option!). Come late October or early November, he would undergo a metamorphosis in his behaviour. Instead of being merely apathetically drunk, he would set about doing damage to property to the extent that the police (who, like the townsfolk generally, normally had a very tolerant attitude to his usual pranks) just had to take action and charge him. If he got his timing right, his spell inside would nicely cover the holiday period and maybe see him through the worst of the winter as well, so that he could walk out as the buds were starting to spring forth.

I wasn't often called to Magistrates' courts to give evidence in the later years, but one fine late September morning found me there, sitting on the still-familiar benches waiting for my case to come up. Into the ordered quiet of the court there erupted a sound of shouting, struggling and swearing coming from the corridor outside. The door burst open and in came Jimmy, arms flailing and legs kicking out as he tried to throw off the policemen and a court official who, clinging to him like terriers, were trying to stop him. They were having no real success at it, for Jimmy was a strong lad and had enough drink in him to give him the strength of ten, so to speak.

"Imhannotioths!" came from him; he was at the well-slurred-syllable stage of intoxication, and considering how he could present himself almost reasonably at alcohol levels which would have had any God-fearing citizen on his back, what he'd taken to get like this beggared belief. As it happened, they were on the point of calling his case anyway and as his progress, however disorderly, had landed him sprawling in the dock, it seemed appropriate just to get on with things.

The charge was read out.

"How do you plead, guilty or not guilty?" said the magistrate, eyeing Jimmy with a coldness born of long familiarity — Jimmy was a regular to every "Beak" on the circuit — just how he was addressed tended to reflect the bench's work-load that day. Today, however, was different.

"Aaayteficouo'tha!" came the well-slurred syllables.

His solicitor stood up and moved over to consult with his client. We couldn't hear what was said, but the non-verbal element was quite unmistakeable. Eventually he turned to the bench, offering the merest flicker of a smile. It was not returned.

"Unfortunately, as you can see, my client is in no fit state to make a proper plea. I must request an adjournment until a more appropriate time."

"Will there be a more appropriate time, do you think?" The face was as deadpan as ever.

"If you could see your way to a fortnight's adjournment, we will do all that we can to see that he presents himself in a better state then."

It was all the assurance he or anyone else could give and was utterly worthless, as everyone knew, but it was a let-out and the reply was well-tinged with relief, even if appearances had to be kept up.

"Very well, then," said the magistrate, "adjourned for two weeks." Then to Jimmy; "You understand that, eh? You come back here, sober, in two weeks, or I shall take a very serious view of the matter!"

Jimmy said nothing, but in response to a prod from one of the policemen beside him, lurched out of the courtroom, the door slamming behind him. A corporate sigh of relief was heaved as the next case was called. The sigh of relief, however, was premature, for almost immediately the corridor was again filled with

155

shouts and roars, together with the noise of things being kicked; then came a bang and the tinkling of broken glass, followed immediately by the deafening ringing of the fire alarm.

Business was once more suspended and the legal contingent in the front began hurriedly to sweep up their papers before evacuating the building. They were stopped in their tracks by one of the police officers, who came in from the corridor, waved for calm and shouted out. "It's all right; it's just Jimmy — he's broken the fire alarm glass!"

The expression on the magistrate's face suggested that, whatever judicial qualities he possessed, they hadn't come with a sense of humour.

My case was next and at the end of it I made my way out, passing the policemen (all of whom I knew pretty well by then) in the corridor.

"What set Jimmy off there?" I asked of one of them.

"Ach, now he was annoyed at only getting a fortnight's adjournment — you see he'll go down for a couple of months and that'll mean he'll be out . . . probably round about Christmas Eve. And that wouldn't suit him at all, you see!"

As I headed for the car, I wondered just how drunk Jimmy had been and I rather suspected he'd taken us all in. Next time he came my way, I would upgrade him to a worthy adversary and match cunning with cunning!

High court, the highest civil court in the province, would never be the scene of the sort of goings-on that occasionally disturbed the tenor of the country courthouses. For a start, the imposing size and architecture would intimidate the most recalcitrant hooligan into respectful acquiescence; second, being a civil court and concerned almost entirely with compensation issues, most of those there were trying to make as good an impression as they could, not wanting to risk a loss of compensation from bad behaviour. Nonetheless, human dramas of a different kind were played out there every day and people left with their expectations satisfied or sometimes dashed, often after years of waiting. For the civil courts are not noted for their speed — it was probably of them that the phrase about the law being "like the mills of God, grinding slow but exceeding fine" was coined.

Senior Counsel came bustling over to me (Senior Counsel seem to bustle everywhere on a court morning, when things become a hive of frenetic activity as deals are struck and the impetus kept up in negotiating, often, several cases at once).

"We've a problem here," he said, taking me by the arm and towing me to one side out of earshot of our clients. "She just wants to settle for what she's been offered and I reckon the case is worth twice as much at least."

This was bit of a reversal of the usual situation, when the plaintiff, convinced that his case is worth many times what he's been offered, takes up a lot of legal time and effort being brought into the realms of reality and persuaded to take what's been negotiated.

"It seems she's got some secret she doesn't want to have made public and she won't talk about it to anyone; will you have a go?"

"She never mentioned anything untoward when I saw her," I said. "She's hardly likely to spill a load of intimate detail to me, here and now — but sure, I'll talk to her."

I had seen her over a year earlier to provide a report for the case, a straightforward claim arising from a road accident some months earlier, but that had been my only contact with her. Seeing her again, I was struck by the change in her: a year ago she had seemed a normal, even attractive, lass of forty-something, if rather quiet in her manner. Today she looked almost gaunt, her slightly sunken eyes accentuating the "hunted" look that seemed to cloak her and govern her whole body language. She'd also lost a lot of weight.

Her wan smile of greeting was brief, but almost forced.

"I can't go into court, Doctor — I just can't," she blurted out, "and nothing you say can make me!" She was not going to be persuaded.

"Why not?" I asked. "Nobody's going to eat you, and from what I gather you're going to sell yourself short if you go on like this."

"If I go in there, it'll all come out; I know it will."

"What will come out? Look — you can tell me and I can promise it won't go any further; whatever it is, we can maybe find a way around it."

Her eyes filled with tears. "There's no way around it . . . I'm dying, and if I go into court *he*'ll find out."

158

This was out of the blue — I'd assumed that she'd committed some indiscretion whose disclosure would have embarrassed her, but this was a bombshell. I gathered my wits enough to ask; "*Who'll* find out?"

"My husband — you see, I've never told him; he thinks I'm just a bit run down and it would be terrible if he found out in court when he's just sitting listening there." She clutched my arm. "Please don't tell him — please!"

I could at least assure her of that — after all, I'd never met her husband and wasn't going to begin an acquaintance by blurting out a tragic, foolishly kept secret of that order.

The first words having been spoken, the rest came almost freely: she began to explain that around the time I'd first seen her she'd been diagnosed with a malignancy (she couldn't tell me exactly what, but I suspected it was something out of the ordinary run of such things and particularly aggressive). It had been quite widespread by the time it was picked up and radical treatment was out of the question: she had refused other treatment, believing (probably correctly) that it would simply give a poorer quality to what time she had left.

I persuaded her to let me talk to her Senior Counsel.

"Good God!" He was visibly shaken. "And she hasn't even told her husband?" He scratched his head where it showed under the edge of his wig. "Well, it does at least explain it after a fashion — wouldn't you think he'd be the first to be told? Still, we both know people do very funny things, eh?"

In these strange circumstances Counsel adopted the best tactic that he could — he pressed the negotiations as if he'd be prepared to go into court and fight it all the way, got a much better offer and took it when they were on the point of "going in".

I left, my duties over, wondering, not for the first time, at the way people behave under stress.

Inevitably I lost contact with the participants, although I heard indirectly that, strangely, she'd lived on long enough to outlive the marriage.

Or perhaps not so strangely.

CHAPTER
SIXTEEN

Too Close

It was one of those glorious, all-too-rare days that show Ulster at its best — not a cloud in the sky, the sun high and hot: just the day to be off work. The only small fly (well, large fly) in the ointment was that I was on call that evening. "Ah, well," I thought, "maybe the patch will be quiet tonight — at least 'til the Sundowners start ringing in."

As usual, optimism in these matters is just that; it was still broad day when the phone rang.

"Doctor, I wonder could you come out and see Hugh O'Rourke? He's collapsed."

No arguing about that one then — no "come down to the surgery tomorrow" for this.

At least the directions sounded simple: "Turn right at the crossroads, pass the third house on the left and down a wee short lane to the house." Crisp, clear and easy, although it was a good ten-mile drive into the hills.

For once the directions were as good as they had sounded and I turned into the little lane, one I hadn't noticed before and more than half-hidden by the "Third House on the Left". Twenty or so yards down, the lane ended beside a cottage of whose existence I'd had no idea until now, despite the countless times I'd passed the hidden lane end. Of good solid stone with a slate roof (no penny-pinching here), it would have graced any calendar picture; a bit of ground in front of it, roses round the door, a garden, more or less tidy, beside it and by the door a long bench, of the sort beloved by primary schools and impoverished church halls. Sitting on it was an elderly man, stocky, simply but tidily dressed, looking me over with a friendly grin on his face.

"Mr O'Rourke?" I asked.

"Aye, that's me." The voice was clear and strong, the smile even broader.

"I thought you'd collapsed — didn't know if I was going to find you alive."

"Ach, now Doctor, it was nought but a wee dwam — I'm right as rain now. I told them not to go dragging you out all this way for me — I'm rightly now."

(I was warming to this chap already — if they don't want to see you, chances are that there's something significant amiss.)

"Tell me what happened, anyway."

"Ach, man dear, I just stood up a bit too quick and got a bit dizzy — I went down til the floor for a whean o' minutes — but I'm fine now — as it happened Bridget next door was here and I think she panicked a bit — I'm rightly now, so I am."

So my first job was to convince him that he needed to be looked over, despite his protestations.

162

Still, it was a glorious evening: the sun shone across the whole of his view — and what a view! He was about eight hundred feet above the level of the lough, six or seven miles away, with nothing to interrupt his view as far as the hills along the coastline, nearly thirty miles away. The Broad Lough, perspective narrowing it to a band of silver, was the focus of the middle ground, the slopes of the foreground dominated by masses of broom in full golden flower; the only sound was of bees working around the bushes.

We started to talk, not so much about the episode which had brought us into contact, but about all sorts of things — "Of shoes and ships and sealing wax and cabbages and kings". He did most of the talking, for a new face is always welcome to a storyteller.

We ranged into politics, a subject I usually steered well clear of. "What must an Englishman like yourself think of the likes of us, that can't live together in a lovely place like this without fighting an' killing 'other, eh?" He'd worked, like so many others, in England in his younger days, returning to the family cottage to "pass his time in rest and quietness". Now in his early eighties, his stories went back to before the Easter Rising and the troubled years that followed; as well as that, he was extraordinarily well informed on current affairs, gleaning his information from his transistor radio (the house, for all its proximity to the road, had no electricity — "I never really felt a call for it" was his comment).

We sat watching the evening turn to gold then pink and I suddenly remembered why I was there.

163

"You know, now I'm here I really ought to get a look at you, if only to keep Bridget happy."

"Ach sure, if ye like."

But I had left it a bit too late — the inside of the house was now too dark for the subtleties of clinical examination and however agreeable a soul he was I could hardly ask him to strip off and stretch out on the bench in the sunset. I had noted, however, that he seemed quite pale, and I had already formed the idea that he was more than a bit anaemic. The chat had revealed that he "hadn't the energy" for the garden and found a lot of previously easy tasks "a bit of a trial now, Doctor."

"I think I should take a wee bit of blood from you and have it checked — if I do it now it'll save the nurse having to come out tomorrow."

The room, furnished as it might have been for the past two centuries, was so dark that I had to find syringe, needle, bottle and the other paraphernalia largely by touch and familiarity with the contents of the bag. But to find the vein I really needed a light. There were a few glowing embers of turf on the hearth (probably from boiling the kettle at tea time — the fire with its crane, the kettle hanging from it on its chain, seemed the only means of cooking in the house). I found a piece of dry hay and knelt before the ashes, blowing them gently to a patch of bright red. The wisp of hay caught and in the second or two of flame I had a candle lit; sticking it on the table in a saucer which seemed to have spent its life as a candle holder, I was able to find a vein and draw off the blood I needed. I

164

wondered, as I did all this, what my academic urbane teaching hospital teachers would have thought. The young "clever" ones would have been contemptuous, but I suspect many of the older ones might just have envied me.

I felt I had to go, for I'd been away far longer than we'd ever imagined I'd be; God knows what work was piling up for me — the Sundowners would be queuing by now.

"What on earth kept you so long?" was Alice's response when I rang in to check on any further calls in the neighbourhood. "Was he dead or what?"

"No, far from it — I think he was more alive than I am."

It was no surprise when the blood test revealed a marked iron-deficiency anaemia; in an eighty-odd-year-old this is always worrying, as gastro-intestinal malignancy is high on the list of possible causes.

However, when he'd been fully investigated I realised I'd missed the one important clue, because I'd been too close to it. The crane over the turf fire carried a kettle but there was no cauldron or pot of any kind to be seen. It turned out that he lived on tea and bread with so little iron in his diet that he'd simply slid into a primary iron-deficiency anaemia over the years. Fortunately, putting that right is kids' stuff these days, so he soon got back to his garden. I hope he grew plenty of spinach!

CHAPTER
SEVENTEEN

The Art of Communication

Much is written these days about the art of communicating your advice to your patients; indeed, budding general practitioners are now formally assessed on their abilities in that field. What nobody does is assess the competence of the patient in passing information the other way.

"I am troubled with a Hair Nail in my stomach" — I stalled on this one, conjuring up some surreal, Dali-esque vision of — well, of just what I couldn't work out; until I did, there seemed little point in reading the letter further. It had come in with the usual daily assortment of requests, dealing with which was part of the routine after the last morning surgery patient had left, along with signing piles of repeat prescriptions and Sickness Certificates, the latter mainly for those who'd been off work so long they'd forgotten any other way of life.

For many, writing to the practice is almost the only time they commit their thoughts to paper and as with so much of the rest of their lives, economy is the watchword; letters come, more often than not, on a quarter sheet of cheap notepaper or exercise book, carefully torn to straight edges. I often wonder what becomes of the other three-quarters: one to the milkman, one to the neighbour who does the shopping and one to . . . well, your guess is as good as mine — at least it's not big enough to hang up in the lavatory!

"Please can you send me more Orovite (a compound, and quite expensive, vitamin preparation) for a month, for Mrs . . .?" This one rang a bell — I felt sure I'd written something very similar only a short while earlier. Perhaps time was flying faster as I was getting older.

"Let me just check her card, will you?" I asked the receptionist (at that time the word "computer" had not entered the language, let alone the practice). The instinct was right — an identical request barely ten days earlier and more odd still, a string of similar ones going back many months, all authorised by others in the practice, so that no one had realised just how much of the stuff was pouring into that particular household.

"No more of that until I find out what's going on; after all, it's not as if there's a huge pocket of beri-beri or something out there; besides, if she's eating all this herself she could be laying up trouble."

A day or two later, I was out in the area — a land of undulating pasture with scattered, mainly mixed, small farms. As I had a few minutes to spare I detoured down the lane to the little cottage which passed for the farmhouse.

167

Mrs . . . 's daughter opened the door to me, as surprised to see me as was her mother when I entered the kitchen living room. The scene was straight out of the nineteenth century; an earthen floor, a settle drawn up in front of a glowing turf fire over which hung a pot on its blackened crane. None of this was much out of the ordinary at that time. What was unusual was that the space between the settle and the fire was taken up by a large and seemingly contented sow, stretched out and enjoying the warmth as she suckled her many offspring — well, all but one of her many offspring: that little piggy was lying on Mrs . . . 's lap with all the innocence of a small baby; indeed, for a split second I thought I'd missed out on a domiciliary delivery in the preceding weeks.

Mrs . . . was feeding it, with all the care and attention she'd have bestowed on one of her own species, from a dropper, of a type that looked only too familiar. Beside the settle stood the corroborating evidence — a bottle of Orovite, its dropper cap off.

"I was just passing and I thought I'd better call in and see what you were doing with all the Orovite," I said.

She at least had the grace to look guilty. "Ah, well . . . y'see . . . we've had a few poor litters recently an' I thought it would give the wee ones a mite better chance if they got some vitamins into them."

I pointed out that NHS was National Human Service and that we couldn't really take on pigs (or anything else on four legs) as well. I rather think she spotted a degree of ambivalence in my tone, as well as the fact that I was not quite keeping a straight face during the lecture. I think that helped us to part friends, although I kept my outburst of giggling until I was well into the car and leaving the yard.

We had no more requests after that, but it became yet another image to suppress when defending the Irish to our English friends.

"Doctor, I'm up four times a night and can't sleep. Also using Electric bill." (When I first read it, it looked like: "Also using Electric drill" — which could at least have explained his insomnia, at the risk of inducing another fit of surrealism in the reader.) As it was, this boiled down to a request for sleeping tablets, things we handed out with what, today, would seem gay abandon.

One request arrived on my desk in casualty with the rest of the day's mail: addressed in a shaky, aged hand, the (reused) envelope bore insufficient postage and a postmark from about thirty miles away. Intrigued, I opened it and drew out a fragment, something under half, of a sheet of cheap writing paper. On it was a message: "Please send anvilis to Johnny Mallon, for hes not well this long time."

Hardly a 999 job, then. The main problem was that while there was a name, the writer had forgotten to add an address: even in rural Ulster this is a major omission, so some detective work was needed. We set about ringing all the practices in the area covered by the postmark (a much smaller one than today; today, you'd be ringing around the whole Province) to see if they could identify the writer. In a very short time we found a receptionist who not only knew of the people concerned, but was able to tell us that he'd been admitted to a neighbouring hospital almost a week beforehand. I presume that he was taken there in the "anvilis", whoever arranged it for him.

All in a morning's work, I suppose.

It's not just written requests that can bring you up short.

The department had not been particularly busy and as afternoon drew on towards tea-time and the end of another working day, barring emergencies, I was winding down, tidying up paperwork for the following day (yes, it *was* a long time ago — today you'd be lucky to be doing last week's paperwork today), when the external phone rang.

"Can you send an ambulance out for Johnny Mullins at Glenarvil? He's broken his back!"

"Right, I'll do that, just give me the details of where you are and I'll pass the message on to the driver." (I wondered why they hadn't dialled 999 instead of ringing the hospital direct, but with that sort of story you don't waste time on formalities.)

"What happened to him — did he fall?" I asked.

"No, no; he was having a bath and when he got out and was drying himself down he saw that his back was broken: ye'd need to hurry, doctor!"

Another attack of surrealism had set in. I tried to keep a serious voice, for after all I hadn't seen the lad yet — but at those few words I'd already downgraded this episode several steps. After all, you don't "just

170

notice" that you've broken your back; moreover, even if you had some strange neurological condition that stopped you feeling pain, it would almost certainly stop you having a bath on your own, never mind getting out and drying yourself unaided. The sense of urgency was giving way to curiosity, however, and I decided to stay on until he arrived: it would hardly have been fair to leave this in the hands of the junior doctor on call that night, a young Indian chap who hadn't been in the country all that long and who no doubt still cherished the illusion (as we all did at that stage) that medicine was really quite straightforward, once you had all the facts. He probably still believed what he was told as well and it wouldn't do to disillusion him too suddenly.

Glenarvil is a good step away ("a good step" is anything from half a mile to ten miles and this was nearer the latter than the former), so it was almost an hour before the ambulance returned. The Broken Back, a young lad of fifteen or so, was sitting in a wheelchair. "Well, he walked out to meet us when he heard us coming," said John, who'd driven out for him. "There didn't seem much point in forcing him to lie down — forbye that, he says he gets sick in cars an' he's better off sitting up."

"What happened to you?" I asked the lad.

"Me back's broke," he replied, and before we could stop him, he leapt out of the wheelchair and swung himself up onto the examination couch with all the suppleness you'd expect of a fifteen-year-old.

Examination made my delayed departure worthwhile, for he turned out to have an early but quite definite

171

scoliosis (a developmental twisting of the spine which often comes on at that age and may in some cases progress to a need for surgery). This had obviously been going on for a while but had been unnoticed until he'd caught a glimpse of it in the bathroom mirror and panicked.

At least immediate management was easy, reassurance and a referral to the orthopaedic clinic being all that was required. And my dinner wasn't too much delayed.

The Hair Nail? Ah, yes: after a bit of head scratching and a trawl through his card, we decided he simply needed a new truss for his hernia. Frankly, a Hair Nail would have been much more interesting.

CHAPTER
EIGHTEEN

Pete

Pete was a one-off, even in this land of eccentrics. Age did not weary him and his exploits could fill a book on their own.

Jackie P. swung the ambulance stretcher alongside the emergency trolley; one of the younger generation of ambulance staff, he'd not been with us long but was fitting into the team very nicely — he also had a great way with patients and was never slow to add his penn'orth to the day's craic.

"Doctor," he said as I lent a hand to offload his patient (a non-urgent problem who was just waiting with us until a bed could be found), "have . . . have ye heard of anything going on in Farrenstown this morning?" He pulled me away from earshot of the new arrival. "I've a feeling something bad's happening out there."

"What do you mean, Jacko, 'something bad'?"

In a near-whisper, while he was folding up the blankets, he said, "When we were going out to this, I passed your man, that young doctor — can't mind his name . . ."

"Doctor Pete?"

"Aye, the very one — we saw him going out of town and . . . he had two coffins on the roof and another one sticking out of the boot — I feel something awful's going on, Doc."

"Well, well — didn't think he was knocking them off in threes, now."

"Threes? That's not the half of it: when we were coming back, there he was again, with four on this time — and definitely not the same ones."

Same ones or not, it doesn't do for the local doctor to be ferrying coffins around singly, let alone in car loads, in broad daylight and I was becoming intrigued.

". . . and I saw some folks crossing themselves as he went past."

"Maybe an outbreak of plague that they want to keep . . . er . . . covered up, if you'll pardon the phrase?"

"D'ye think so . . .?" Then he realised I wasn't being serious.

"I'll find out and tell you, if you haven't heard by then yourself — one or other of us is bound to find out sooner or later."

The day passed without any sign of a Farrenstown Apocalypse, as did the next day.

A couple of days later, I went along to the weekly joint hospital/GP clinical meeting and as luck would have it found that I and Pete's Senior Partner were the first to arrive. We'd been friends for years and as we reached for our second sandwich I remembered Jacko's story.

174

"Tell me, what was I hearing about Pete shifting coffins the other day? I know half the population thinks we're in the pay of the undertakers, but what I heard sounded well out of the ordinary . . ."

I stopped: the Senior Partner was choking on his mouthful of sandwich. "Jasus, Hughie, that's what I was going to tell you — nearly forgot. Let's say it's true but you need the background.

"Monday morning, yer man gets an urgent call to the town centre to a man we know well — been on the Broo[1] for years but working away out of sight y'know. Pete gets down there, finds him in a rare state of panic. Seemed he'd been tipped off that the boys from the Broo Office were coming to pay him a surprise visit. Now this oul' boy makes all the coffins for the local undertakers — decent professional jobs they are too; you'd be quare an' comfortable in one of his boxes. Howanever, someone had tipped the wink to the Broo and Investigating Officers were to pay a call.

"'If they find all this stuff I have out the back, I'm done for,' he says to Pete. 'What can I do? I can trust you, Doc.'

"So yer man scratches his head and says, 'Right, right, leave it to me,' and heads off home, makes a few phone calls, puts the roof rack on the car and starts shipping the bloody coffins out to safe houses all round the countryside, while the fellow's tidying the place up and making it look like he only does a bit of woodwork as a hobby, like.

---

[1] On the Broo: receiving unemployment benefit.

"I'd have minded less if I hadn't had to do his surgery as well as mine: I didn't get the visits started until near two o'clock. At least he did mine in the evening."

I said, slowly, "I think that's called 'Conspiring to Pervert the Course of Justice', isn't it?"

"Ach, that's the Englishman in you coming out, just when we thought we had it nicely buried!" was all the reply I got.

I laughed. "Not sure I'd have done the same, mind — but you've got to hand it to him for ingenuity!"

". . . and knowing the right people to stash them on," said the Senior Partner, knowingly.

Like many of the local GPs, Pete had begun his career in the local hospital, in his case using the jobs to fine-tune his gloriously eccentric style of practice. On one occasion, when providing weekend cover for, *inter alia*, the casualty department, he called in and, seeing the place quiet, told the Sister-in-charge: "I'm just going for a wee jog; I'll have the bleep with me and I'll not be far away — OK?" Whereupon he headed out into the rain of a blustery February afternoon. (Even then this desertion of one's post was greatly frowned upon; today it would be unthinkable and usually logistically impossible anyway.)

As it was, he'd not been long gone when an unannounced ambulance brought in a trio of victims from a road accident — a mother and young daughter from one car and the driver of the other vehicle. Mother and daughter were placed in the cubicle nearest the door, while the other driver went to the only other free one at the far end. As he needed rather more immediate attention, Sister began dealing with him after sending Pete an urgent bleep.

On hearing the bleep, Pete turned and sprinted back, guilt no doubt lending him wings. Assuming, correctly, that the problem lay in casualty, he ran straight there and through the main door, plunging into the first cubicle he came to.

Now, whatever Pete's virtues were, sartorial elegance was not one of them; indeed, it was out of sight at the bottom of his life's priorities; the effects of a jog in the pouring rain did nothing to improve his overall appearance.

Sister's first intimation of his return was an ear-splitting scream from the first cubicle, a scream loud enough to be heard throughout the hospital, let alone the department. Dropping everything, she rushed to the source of the sound and found Pete standing, a little nonplussed, beside a terror-stricken mother who'd thrown herself over the child to save her from assault by this dripping wet, dirty-mac'd apparition, hair frizzed out on end and sporting a look between the seriously unshaven and the immature beard from which a pair of eyes stared in uncomprehending amazement.

"Oh, it's all right," said Sister, "this is the doctor come to examine you," whereupon she smiled and went back towards her own patient. She'd covered only three or four paces when the awful incongruity hit her and she turned back to try to offer some sort of soothing explanation. As she said later, "She was all right about it in the end, but I think she thought she'd been brought to the madhouse by mistake an' it took her a while to get her composure back."

I bet it did, but this was (and still is to a large degree) a community tolerant of eccentricity; I hope it remains so.

CHAPTER
NINETEEN

The Prime Site

"Would you look in on Seamus Doyle, Doctor?" said the voice at the other end of the phone. "He's not one bit well today."

"Seamus Doyle? Not a name I know — is he one of mine, do you know?"

"I wouldn't know now — he wasn't over fussed on going to doctors. But he needs somebody to see him right and soon."

I was on duty on my own that day, so just whose patient he was didn't really matter anyway. "Sure, I'll see him; where does he live?"

The address was only a few hundred yards away, but didn't make sense. "Do you know the number?" I asked.

"Sure, Doctor, I don't know as if it ever had a number."

Now this was in the main street of the town, which had had numbers for a century or more. "Where exactly is he, then?"

"Next the wee supermarket, as you go out of town."

"But there's only a bit of waste ground there, isn't there?"

"Ah, well, sure it's not much better than waste ground itself, so it is, his place."

As soon as morning surgery was over, I stuck the bag into the car and ran up to the far end of the main street as far as the little shop that called itself "supermarket" (a new term in the country then, though there was little of the super about it). Just past it lay an area of waste ground, "A Prime Commercial Site, Ripe for Development", in estate-agent-speak. I had to look at it in detail before I saw that a piece of old wall with a door-sized hole in it had some corrugated iron over it, forming a roof of sorts. It looked like an abandoned pig-house on a derelict farm, not a main-street house in a market town. There were no other contenders for the description, however, and as I walked over towards it a man came out, ducking through the door-sized opening and confirming my feeling that this was indeed my destination.

"Ah, Doctor, he's wild bad — I doubt if he'll do — not that I'm telling you your job, Doctor, you'd be the one to know," he added in apology for his diagnostic temerity. He turned and came back into the house with me, giving me the chance to smile and disclaim omniscience, as we both ducked under the door and into the darkness.

The door seemed the only source of light — if there had ever been a window it had disappeared long ago as the building had slowly fallen down around its occupant.

Of that occupant there seemed at first no sign, although a knock-me-down-powerful smell of excrement made me glad I had a few seconds to gather myself to become professional and business-like.

180

Eventually I made out a mattress on the floor. The floor itself was of earth and the mattress, filthy and rotten, appeared to be blending itself with the ground and slowly returning to its elements. Beside the mattress was what appeared to be the only other object in the room, an old tin bucket full almost to the brim with urine and faeces and at least the immediate source of the smell.

The sharp end of medical practice makes you a connoisseur of smells, most of them repulsive in their own ways but occasionally diagnostic. One of my old teachers used, probably too often, the command: "Examine the pus: dear me — you don't need a laboratory to tell you that smells of Coliform" (or Staph, or Strep, or whatever was the subject of his diatribe). Mind, he'd never stick his nose into a bottle of fresh urine for a deep sniff as his medieval predecessors might have done; as far as doing the same to a bucket of turds, I suspect that a cautious stir with a long stick while standing well upwind would have been his limit — that *was* for the lab. Still, something must have rubbed off (maybe I should re-phrase that), for I always made a good sniff a regular part of the consultation process.

The mattress smelt of more mature excreta, slowly reverting to the earth around it; but there was also a smell of death, as if the living body before me was already beginning to disintegrate even before life itself snuffed out.

He lay, he who was and for a very short time more would be, Seamus Doyle; a shell of a man, the eyes sunken and barely open, saliva caked upon his lips and mouth out of which, with scarcely any movement, came an incoherent noise, a mix of groan and mumble: if he was saying anything, no one on Earth would understand it. I pulled down the one blanket covering him and had a look at his belly. There would be no detailed diagnosis here; the first one, "Is he sick?" was already answered; "Can I do anything for him here and now?" (probably not, unless a large dose of morphine to make his passing easier could be squared with the GMC); "Can we get him to anyone who *could* help?" (probably many months or even years too late for that); "Can I make him more comfortable while I try to sort out something?" (But what? Short of the morphine, probably very little.)

All these thoughts were passing through my mind (along with the more obvious one of, "How the hell did he slide down into this state in the first place?"), as I looked at the distended, rigid abdomen. It seemed tender only because the moaning mumble increased a bit as I gently began to poke around. Pulling the blanket all the way down gave me a diagnosis and the answers to all my questions in an instant; in the lower part of the belly a large red raised area was dribbling faeces and mucus from its rotten black centre. So that was it, almost certainly a bowel malignancy with a fistula through the belly wall and leakage into the peritoneal cavity giving him an almost certainly terminal peritonitis. The morphine was beginning to look like the best option for him after all. But not just yet; after all, I hardly knew him.

I stepped outside, bringing his visitor with me.

"How in God's name did he get into this state, then?" I asked in a low voice, although the chance of being overheard was nil. "Has nobody seen him about this?"

I realised I was speaking more sharply than I should have been; after all, the fellow was doing him a favour just by looking in on him — so I ended with a more gentle, "Do you know if anybody's been in with him?"

"Not to my knowing, Doctor — he was an awfu' thrawn sort of a man and wouldn't go near any of yous — not for years that I know of." His voice lowered to a confidential near-whisper: "Between you an' me, Doctor, I think he was afeared of yous all — thought he might have something really bad and didn't want to know."

"Well, he wasn't wrong there — I think you're right, he hasn't much longer to go: I'll see what can be done to make things easier for him."

At times like this it's useful to be on good terms with the admitting staff at the local hospital; as soon as I returned to the surgery I spoke to the one on duty, explaining the story and warning him that he'd only need the bed for a day or so. Then I picked up the rest of the day where I'd left off — this had cost me quite a bit in time, but he was by far the sickest patient of the day — indeed, they don't come any sicker than that.

An hour or so later the phone rang. "Doc." The warm friendly voice of Jack, one of the ambulance drivers, came over the line. "Doc, we went out for your man in the shack in the main street there. I'm afraid we were too late, he's gone."

"Thanks for letting me know — I'll need to talk to the coroner before we can do anything, but I'll see to it."

I rang the coroner and told him all I knew of the story.

"It's amazing in this day and age that that sort of thing can still happen," he commented. "But I get them regularly from all over my patch — and I'm sure all of us do. Right, I'll take it over."

And so he did, and I rather lost track of what became of the remains. I imagine they had the modern equivalent of a burial on the Parish, public funds being found to defray the minimum cost of interment.

It seemed only a few weeks later that I saw the area cleared and foundation trenches being dug — the Prime Site was already being developed.

CHAPTER
TWENTY

The One-Breath House

Most of the houses on the practice were clean and tidy in varying degrees: there were the positively palatial, houses in which you felt that, if you sat down, you'd have been the first to do so in the place and that even your smart casual professional look was little more than shabby in such surroundings. Perfectly manicured lawns led inside to perfectly manicured carpets; pristine furniture occupied pristine rooms, rooms which had never been seen by, let alone invaded by, a family of boisterous kids hell-bent on turning it into a battlefield. At times I envied these establishments, although their occupants never seemed as happy and content as they should have been. But then, "tidiness does not contentment make", if I may misquote someone or other, and the near-obsessive neatness was as often as not a symptom of a personality living under stress. (So all of you who haven't rearranged the cushions or assiduously swept the furthest corners of the kitchen this morning, take heart — it's just the sign of a balanced personality.)

Most houses, of course, were not like this, being simply ordinary decent homes where families got on with the business of living, paying only such attention to order and regimentation as was necessary for comfort. They formed by far the greater part of the practice — and, worthy as they were, were quite forgettable.

At the far opposite end of the spectrum were those houses that were just so awful that there's very little in ordinary day-to-day vocabulary to do them descriptive justice.

These were not found, as you might think, in the old traditional cottages with their earthen floors and open-hearth turf fires; though often sadly restricted in material possessions, many of these places were so spotless that, "Sure, ye could take yer dinner off o' the floor, so ye could," as I've heard remarked more than once of some of them. To be sure, there were a few grubby ones among them, but fewer than the stranger might think.

No, the really awful ones were for the most part council houses, distinguished from their decent (and no doubt despairing) neighbours by the wilderness that had once, in the hands of previous tenants, been a neat cottage garden: the path, of broken concrete (how the hell do you break up a concrete front path without malice aforethought, I ask you?), through whose parted fragments grass was growing, kept in check, like any other grass on the property, by constant trampling from squads of small and not-so-small children. External decoration was either absent or a long-neglected

186

hangover from the previous tenants, while on the woodwork and the windows grubbiness reigned.

Inside things usually got worse, for these people were strangers to the concept of neatness, the chaotic interior of the house often reflecting the dysfunctional nature of their lives, a dysfunction which in its varied manifestations brought us into all-too-frequent contact. One thing the inside had that was lacking outdoors was the smell. It is said that of all the senses, smell is the most powerfully evocative, even a whiff conjuring up instantly and vividly memories otherwise long buried. As far as I'm concerned I'd prefer those particular ones to stay that way — buried and far from evocation levels.

A headily nauseating concoction, the smells had in them features common to all of these dwellings: old food (on the cooker and trodden into the floor), rancid sweat fermenting under never-removed clothing, unwashed and un-house-trained animals (there was usually a dog around somewhere) and unattended small and incontinent children.

Every practice, everywhere, has places like this and it's more than likely that Ireland has fewer than many of the deprived urban parts of Britain, but out of these we formed the notion of the "One-Breath House", where the ambition was to enter, examine, diagnose, prescribe and leave, all without drawing a breath after entering. It was of course an unattainable ideal, but having laid down the principle, at least you could see how far you could approach it. Even within this gruesome category there was a hierarchy, however.

One such, testifying to the notion of squalor as a reflection of dysfunction, was the site of a visit at least three times a week. As the small bungalow contained a huge number of folks of assorted ages (the most I totted up at one visit was nineteen — not bad for a tiny two-bedroom bungalow), including a son who was severely mentally handicapped, some increased frequency of contact was unavoidable, although in today's parlance they'd probably be termed "multiple heartsinks". Their proximity to the practice meant that they had no hesitation in calling in: "Would you just take a wee race round to see . . .?" The idea that the able-bodied ones of the tribe could take the same "wee race round" to see us never seemed to occur to them, despite unsubtle suggestions to that effect.

Granny presided over the ménage, usually seated on an armchair, the sole survivor of an ancient three-piece suite. On an adjacent, non-matching sofa (at least I think it was non-matching — it was so soiled that the colour had long been indistinguishable and only a minor difference in contour marked it out as not of the same set) lay the handicapped son. Of all the family, he seemed to be the only one who received anything like proper attention, for, helpless as he was, he was almost always reasonably clean and as tidily dressed as you could expect in the circumstances. All the care and "normal" management in the family seemed to have been funnelled onto him, to the entire neglect of the rest. It was doubly sad that the recipient of all this care was incapable of recognising it, while those who were went untended. Perhaps this made us more tolerant of their other abuses of the service than we might otherwise have been, for it showed that there was an underlying humanity as they cared for one whom many another, far better placed to afford and to provide for him, would have unhesitatingly put into care and conveniently forgotten. It was a small sweetener to a bitter pill.

There was never anywhere to set down the bag; the seating always held loads of old clothing, while the feeling of the carpet, or what was left of the carpet, sticking to your shoes made the floor a poor second choice. I usually ended up trying to balance it on edge somewhere, to minimise contact.

Of the many, many visits I made there, it is one of the early ones which stands out. I had seen and attended to one of the eternal crop of toddlers which added their own brand of mayhem to the place, conducting the examination in one of the bedrooms. The short corridor linking it to the living area gave access to the bathroom/toilet adjacent: never too elaborate in its décor, it had been subject to the attentions of one of the toddlers, either my patient or one of its innumerable half-siblings, who had marked a low-set dado line along the wall. It was a pity that he had done so after grubbing about in the contents of a well-filled nappy — the brown didn't even match and the application, while enthusiastic, had been, shall we say, uneven. I steered a course dead on the centre line of the passageway, keeping the bag before me all the way. In front of me, the open bathroom door revealed a handbasin piled with dirty nappies, still awaiting even

189

the first attention — at least you could trace the trail, so to speak.

The examination over, I gathered up my kit.

"Would you like to wash your hands, Doctor?" The invitation was unexpected. I thought of the washbasin and its contents and, in the immortal phrase, "I made an excuse and left".

I was never invited to do so again.

It's funny how the ordinary and decent, unless turning up in a wholly unexpected situation, is not entered into memory — presumably precisely because it *is* ordinary and decent — while the gross stays with you for ever.

Bridget was a single girl. While this was little wonder, she had not lacked for attention in her time, even if the attentions had all been very short-lived. She and her father occupied a small terrace house in the next village. It was easy to find, for, like the overcrowded bungalow, the level of neglect was apparent at a distance. Inside at least there were no toddlers to contribute to the chaos — which was just as well, for Bridget and her dad did chaos very well without other assistance.

Father had had a stroke years ago and slept in the bath (yes, I know it's a non sequitur and I don't know why he slept in the bath: it would have been easier to sleep on the ramshackle sofa which was almost the only piece of furniture in the living room, but he slept in the bath — perhaps he felt safer in it, less likely to fall out of it). Sleeping there also kept him away from the attentions of the dog, who seemed to spend his days chained up in the kitchen, even when his need to go out was manifest and urgent. The results of this unmet need were rarely cleaned up, but in time came to blend with the floor, providing me with yet another sticky surface to contact as little as possible.

The dog was not the only quadruped in the house. For reasons which again were quite unfathomable, Bridget's kitchen always had in it a couple or so sacks of what looked like barley grain. In some of the houses I knew, I'd have been pretty certain that this was the raw material for poteen. Here, however, it seemed out of the question, for Father was not physically capable of a job like that, while as for Bridget, her whole time was spent doing . . . well, nothing, and she certainly lacked the ability to cope with anything remotely as demanding as poteen making.

The other quadrupeds in the place, smaller, furry and with long, scaly tails, were more enterprising and had made great inroads on the sacks through holes at floor level. At least it stopped them attacking the captive dog or the immobile father; after a session at the sacks, they'd be too full to do anything but add their droppings to the general mess before retiring for the night.

District nurses, Social Services, public health officials and rat-catchers had all made their ways to Bridget at one time and another and had all left the place better than when they'd found it — for a short time; then things would revert to her norm and the whole cycle would start again.

It's a free country, I suppose, and folks can live as they like; sometimes it would be nice if some of them could live a little more as we'd like. Still, they contribute colour, if nothing else — and it usually is nothing else.

Farming is a mucky business, but most of the farming community manage to keep a strict separation between Outside and Inside, the living quarters being no more a reflection of the farmyard than of anywhere else. As with everything else in life, though, there are exceptions.

"Would ye come and see Sammy Carter? He's wild bad th' night."

No further relevant information was forthcoming — even the directions weren't going to get me closer than half a mile to the place, having been no more than a garbled string of references to other houses interspersed with distances described as "a wee way" or "it's only a whean o' yards from there, now". Fortunately, Alice knew the house, or at least the long laneway leading to it, and she had been at the mouth of the lane only that afternoon. She enlightened me:

"They probably saw the car and felt it was time they saw a doctor — I bet it was that that put them in the notion!" And to be fair, this particular crowd would have needed little more reason than that for making a call; the wonder was that I'd not been on the receiving end of a call long ago, but it was now nine o' clock on a winter's night and I was about to be inducted into the ways of the Carters.

Armed with understandable directions from Alice, I set off the eight or nine miles into the country, most of the trip in the pitch darkness of a starless night well away from any clusters of houses that might throw a few glimmers onto the road. Even with the directions I managed to miss the inconspicuous gap in the hedge that was the entrance to the lane, perhaps because it was so hidden by the house at the lane's mouth where the afternoon's call had been. A retracing of the two or three hundred yards located it and I turned in, leaving behind the lights of the house, faint enough and all facing the road.

It was a long, uneven track of a lane, two deep ruts separated by a ridge of mud and grass grown wild up to the height of a tractor axle and therefore well above the bumper level of a small saloon. This was a walking-pace job; it might be fine for a tractor, but a tractor could roll far above boulders which could leave the practice car missing a sump — and it would be a long walk home.

There was a kink in the laneway and as I rounded it I saw a star, low down, twinkling just above hedge height — a guiding light indeed, hovering above, if not a stable, then at least the destination of one not-too-wise man. But there was something odd about the twinkle; it seemed slower than the standard stellar one. As I came closer it rather lost its stellar effect and revealed itself to be nothing more than a light on a pole, hanging by a bit of wire and pulsing "bright; dim; bright; dim". At the same time I became aware of a slow rhythmic thumping sound from somewhere close at hand — and all became clear. I'm insatiably curious about all things mechanical and the noise, emanating from a miserable shed just in from the laneside, demanded attention. I took the torch and wandered into the fenced-off piece of field to peer in through a tiny, filthy window at the source of the sound.

Such light as I had showed that my little excursion had been well worthwhile: grubby, but still resplendent in its black, brass and copper, stood an ancient single-cylinder diesel engine driving an equally ancient dynamo, its progress a cycle of "Suck, Squeeze, Bang, Blow". At each "Bang" the light on the pole brightened, only to dim again during the "Suck", "Squeeze" and "Blow" phases. Presumably in the interests of economy it had been set to run as slowly as possible without stalling; I was soon to find out that this was the governing philosophy in the whole establishment.

A few yards further, on the lane widened out into the farmyard, with precious little change in surface quality. There was a light on in the yard and a half-open door threw a further shaft of light onto the scene, all pulsing in surreal synchrony with the lamp on the pole, at a frequency which was low enough to set my head nodding in time with it, before I caught myself on and entered the living room via the shaft of light.

The farmyard continued more or less unabated into the room, the mud of the former barely diminished by the threshold. Furniture was of the sparsest — a couple of old wooden chairs, their original colour long lost under a thick patina of grime; a plain wooden table which appeared not to have been cleared or cleaned since it was bought, bearing upon it a teapot, a jug of milk and a bowl, all of them filthy, the darkening crusting around their rims a testament to a lack of attention between refills. The smell of the place was . . . no, forget it.

Despite this, the bowl, or at least its content, was being assiduously attacked by a youth of anything between thirteen and sixteen. Basic table manners had evidently not reached this neck of the woods and his efforts were directed at moving the contents of the bowl into his mouth as quickly as was possible. They say people come to resemble their pets or the animals they work with; if this is so, then there was no doubt that this lad was already well-settled into the business of pig-farming. Not only were his manners those of the trough, but as I looked I could already see the beginnings of a physical resemblance, the nose stubby and blunt-ended, the eyes close together and focused near-sightedly on the task in hand. Neither he nor his mother, standing by the table watching him, acknowledged my arrival in any formal way, but Mother spoke up as I planted my bag on the table (well, it was the cleanest, or at least the least dirty place I could see and I didn't think they would mind, considering the state of the floor).

"See, I told you I'd get the doctor in to you if you didn't eat yer tea, now, didn't I?" Then to me: "Doctor, this lad won't eat his meat, whatever I put before him; ye'd need to give him something."

Sammy was giving the lie to his mother's complaint by shovelling the bowl's contents into himself at a speed which would have done credit to a small digger and in the few seconds since my entrance had almost cleaned it. Thoughts crowd in on one at times like this, such as:

"If I'd been given that, I'd have unhesitatingly puked any prior stomach contents around it." Or:

"If he's not eating, it's the best thing that he could do." (Sammy was no lightweight and could well have done with a period of starvation.) Or:

"If he'd refuse *that*, it'd probably be one of the wiser moves he's made today."

Only then, the obvious thought: "Have I been dragged out here at night to give dietary advice to one who doesn't need it and probably wouldn't give a toss about it if it were given?"

A lecture on the inappropriateness of such a call was tempered by the knowledge that I was wasting my breath and, just a little bit, by the fact that I now knew where to lay my hands on a nice antique diesel generating set — if they ever got around to having the mains installed.

The headlights of the car seemed so nice and steady on the way home, after that.

CHAPTER
TWENTY-ONE

Beginnings and Endings

It was my morning for one of my routine surgical lists, and while the Staff Nurse was setting up theatre, removing instruments from the sterilising drums (which, hot from the oven, were contributing clouds of steam to the theatre atmosphere) and generally bustling around, I went to the office to do a bit of paperwork until we were ready to start.

The office stood adjacent to the car park and the ambulance entrance, but its frosted windows allowed no view to the outside. A few minutes into the paperwork, I was interrupted by the sound of a vehicle, not an ambulance, coming into the area at high speed. The fact that the car park was a cul-de-sac, closed off by a massive stone wall, made me prick up my ears in anticipation of the sound of breaking glass and crumpling metal as the consequence of a serious misjudgement manifested itself. But no; a violent braking to the sound of protesting tyres seemed to bring it up short somewhere by the ambulance entrance. I had the scene in my mind's eye: "Clunk — that's the door being slammed";

"swish, clatter — the entrance door swinging shut"; "tap, tap, tap — footsteps: are they coming my way?"

Only it wasn't "tap, tap, tap" — it was a pell-mell clatter of hob nails on terrazzo and it was definitely coming my way. The desperate bellow: "Doctor, doctor!" confirmed the bad news and I saw another ordered morning dissolving into all-too-familiar chaos.

I rose and went out of the office to meet the source of the shout.

"Doctor, come quick — the wife's having a baby in the car!" Almost grabbing me, he towed me towards the entrance, giving me no time to organise, or indeed to think of anything except that over the years I'd managed to suppress all thoughts of obstetrics and now I was too old to be gathering them together again. Uncharitably, I thought, "Just my bloody luck — another five minutes and I'd have been in theatre, scrubbed; then it would have been Anne's problem." (Anne, one of my colleagues, was to do the session in the department while I was otherwise engaged, but she had not yet arrived.) This, I fear, was the predominant thought in the ten-yard dash to the door.

Hard by the entrance stood a Humber "Super Snipe" of the early fifties; though getting on in years by then, they were still a byword for smooth luxury travel — more to the immediate point, they were roomy; even if those who'd designed the roominess had not done so with this sort of eventuality in mind, it looked as if the space was going to come in handy. Mother was on the back seat, obviously well into labour; indeed, I could see the baby's head just beginning to appear. No time then to wheel her along to Maternity — I was just going to have to get on with it here.

"Go you back to where you met me: go straight on and you'll see the reception desk — tell them I need a midwife team down here NOW!"

Glad to be doing anything other than an agitated jig behind me, the father obediently sprinted off, leaving me to "assist". As it turned out, little assistance was needed, for several reasons: she already had three children, but this one had come prematurely, so delivery was likely to be easier for her; she was already on the point of delivering, so little more than support was needed; and, above all, there was space to move around and get myself into the best position to help, thanking God the while that it wasn't one of the then newly-popular minis — there were by then limits to my suppleness and a Mini would have tested them beyond endurance.

Speedy though the midwives were, Mother beat them to it and I was able to hand over a tiny, but otherwise healthy-looking baby to them as they raced up with trolley and incubator. Midwives are an amiable crowd, but they can be terribly territorial and always Know Best (in my case a safe enough assumption). I got the sort of look that said, "All right, you can go now — we're the professionals here!" as, very professionally indeed, they went about their job, whisking Mother, Baby and Father off to their own domain in no time at all.

Fine by me.

Although it seemed to have taken ages, the whole episode from start to finish had occupied only about ten minutes. I strolled round the corner to see if preparations for the list were complete. Even though she had been no further away from the action than I had been, the intervention of a thick wall and the clatter of the instruments had left the Staff Nurse wholly oblivious to the activity.

"Do you know," I said, as casually as I could, "I've just delivered a baby at the Ambulance entrance."

Her face was much less forgettable than the noise of a dropped trayful of instruments.

The weekend after that was "our" weekend on call for the practice; a weekend typical of an Ulster summer — overcast, the clouds occasionally black enough to make the threat of rain very real (although at least the rain is warmer in summer). A remarkably quiet Sunday was ended by a call; it was Irene.

"Doctor, I'm sorry to bother you, but I wonder if you'd mind coming out to see Colin some time today — he's had a cold on him this good while and it seems to be settled on his chest."

Colin had slipped out of my mind in the time since I'd first seen him — indeed, I'd had no contact with either him or Irene for almost two years, although I'd heard that both were doing well in their respective ways: Irene remained symptom-free and Colin, after the major trauma of surgery, had picked up his studies where he'd been forced to leave them off and was apparently managing well with his artificial leg. So I was more than willing to call out to see them both.

I was ushered upstairs and realised that I was in the same bedroom where Irene had been at the time of our first disastrous encounter (it seemed half a lifetime ago). In the interval, the other children had flown the nest and Colin had been given the largest of the bedrooms, to give him more space to manage himself.

The story was much as I had gleaned over the phone — a mild flu, then a "chestiness" which had not cleared and was now making him a bit short of breath.

Even at this I wasn't happy; fit young lads don't get chest infections in even an Ulster summer, as a rule.

A few seconds into the examination and I had once again the feeling of despair that I'd had when I first saw his X-ray pictures that morning a couple of years ago.

One side of the chest was obviously full of fluid, a stony-dull note to percussion. I also had the impression that his trachea was slightly deviated from the mid-line, suggesting that the fluid, or whatever underlay it, was pushing the central structures of the chest to one side.

Colin couldn't see me as I was behind him, but Irene saw something cross my face and in that instant I knew that she knew and that all the warnings I'd given her at the time of the diagnosis were suddenly materialising from the back of her mind, to where she'd consigned them when Colin had seemed to do so well.

"I think you've a bit of inflammation there, Colin; we'll need to get a chest X-ray tomorrow to see what's going on and I'll arrange that first thing in the morning."

He seemed content with this and I took my leave, following his mother down stairs and into the living room.

"It's the tumour again, isn't it, Doctor?" Her lips found it hard to form the words and to tell the truth I wasn't much better — professional detachment can only go so far.

"I'd be very suspicious of it, but let's not be too hasty in jumping to that conclusion — we'll get films first." (You can't just cut the lifeline, however tenuous it may have suddenly become, even to one you know as well as Irene.)

Her smile was as much for my benefit — she would Play the Game to the last, too:

"Aye, we'll say nothing yet, eh?"

"No, no; nothing yet, Irene — 'sufficient unto the day' and all that, eh?"

I left slowly and got into the car, taking a moment before moving off. "Sufficient unto the day" — but that day was almost upon them.

I never saw Colin again; my fears turned out to be only too well founded, for he had massive secondary involvement in his lung and chest wall. He was admitted directly from X-ray and given such care as could be given. His decline to oblivion was at a pace which some might call cruel, although I and others might call it merciful.

CHAPTER
TWENTY-TWO

Ménage à Trois

The phone rang in the consulting room as I was in the process of winding up a consultation; intrusion though it was, it provided an excuse to hasten the patient on her way — she was the sort who'd keep you all day, given half a chance.

"There's an urgent call in from Sid McNeill, said the receptionist. "I wanted him to hang on so's you could have a word with him, but he wouldn't wait — said he had to get back to see what was going on: he wants you to go and see Louise. I couldn't get anything more out of him and he just hung up."

Great — a call to someone I'd never met, to a condition or situation I had no prior knowledge of, in the middle of a busy afternoon surgery. All part of the job, I suppose and in truth, although I certainly hadn't met Louise, I had already heard plenty about her — and the sister she lived with. Sid was, at least nominally, the husband of Louise, but I'd gathered over the short time I'd been in the practice that he was there only to work, keep house and run messages for Louise and her sister Millie. The relationships in this household were hinted at but never put into words (after all, no one really knew what went on behind the always-closed curtains, although that phenomenon alone caused a lot of speculation among the neighbours, speculation probably more lurid than the usually simply sordid reality), but it was rumoured that the real relationship was between the two sisters (a sort of multi-dimensional perversion, if you see what I mean) and that Sid was only there to keep up appearances and to be useful.

So off I set, with rumour and gossip as my only preparation for the unknown.

The house was nothing out of the ordinary, one of a group of workers' cottages near a crossroads and like many a hundred others in the country. I knocked but had to repeat the process a couple of times before there was any response. The response was a sound that might have been feet shuffling along a wooden floor, followed by the grating sound of a bolt being withdrawn and the rattle of a safety chain being clumsily unhooked from the door. After all this, the door was slowly opened.

Louise stood there, blinking in the light as it cast aside a little of the darkness of the interior. She shielded her eyes from the light — and well she might, for she stood looking as one who'd been out on a protracted "bender" and hadn't had enough time to sleep it off. Her eyes, screwed up against the light, showed shadows, while bags under her eyelids seemed to extend down to her chin. Her hair was not merely tousled, but looked as if it had not seen grooming or washing for many a long day. The spectral look was only emphasised by the short nightie (too short for one of her age and appearance) which constituted her only garment — at four o'clock in the afternoon. Her fingers, still on the edge of the door, were stained to a mahogany with nicotine.

I introduced myself.

"Ah, come on in, Doctor," she beamed — or came as near to beaming as she ever would. She let me in, closing the door as quickly as she could to avoid lighting up the place for a second longer than was essential. In the near-darkness, she motioned me to go upstairs, explaining that the call had been for her sister who had collapsed and could be neither revived nor lifted by Louise. She'd contacted Sid at work; the rest I knew.

I mounted the darkened stairs slowly, for in a place like this you never know what you might find to put your foot on — or through; Louise followed me closely, so closely that she kept bumping against me. At least that was what I thought at first; it was when the hand began working its way up my thigh that I realised I was being "felt up". Now it's one thing to be groped by some handsome young man in a strictly social situation; it's another matter entirely to be groped by some intoxicated harridan on the stair of a house you're visiting professionally. I quickened my pace realising now why she'd let me go first — politeness had had nothing to do with it.

Millie lay on the floor of the bedroom (I'd suddenly developed a reluctance to go anywhere near a bedroom with her sister in tow, but needs must at times). She was in much the same state as her sister, right down to the shortie nightie, but it took only a few seconds to see that she was simply having an episode of either hysteria or frank histrionics (in hysteria you don't know you're doing it; in histrionics you do). She actively resisted our joint attempts to get her up onto the bed: the heaving and moving around that this involved gave Louise ample opportunity to continue her groping exercises and I felt my backside being given a good going over. Eventually, we dragged her onto the bed, knocking over a waste bin full of cigarette butts in the process. Millie stank of drink, unlike Louise, who merely stank of old fags, neglect and halitosis, although I'm sure that drink was there as well — it was just masked by everything else.

The main problem with both of them was not only, perhaps not even primarily, drink; they had become users of phenobarbitone many years ago and had become addicted to the stuff. With no motivation to come off it and with access to sources of supply outside the practice, getting them to cut down on their consumption was a lost cause, even though it was having a significant effect on their behaviour; as for their social relationships, those had been a lost cause for a long time and were unlikely to improve now even if they suddenly came off everything and led blameless lives ever after.

Having got Millie into bed the next problem was to get her off me, for she seemed to share some of her sister's off-beat affection for me and kept her arms firmly round my neck long after any mechanical need was over. At one point I thought she was going to kiss me, but she either thought better of it or couldn't be bothered to press the matter in the face of determined resistance.

Eventually I worked myself free and tried to take some sort of a history, a process interrupted by Louise fawning over me.

"Ah, now, dear — you've a lovely figure, now — so fine and slim — and such lovely hips — an' what a fine dress that is — shows you to perfection, so it does."

History or no history, it was high time I left: the problem seemed no more than another episode in the story I'd been told previously and I'd settled for histrionics rather than hysteria as the diagnosis. Neither sister was in any state to benefit from a lecture and my main desire was to return to the surgery, which had suddenly become a very attractive place.

That was the first of many encounters with the pair; or perhaps I should say the trio, for Sid contributed his share to the workload, usually more indirectly than directly, being either the bearer of requests and tidings (the tidings usually leading to the requests) or occasionally being the reason for the call-out — not that he was there, or even knew of the call, you understand — he was just the reason for the call.

On one of these visits (I think by then their passion for me had subsided far enough for me to manage a more-or-less normal consultation with them, though I always kept one eye on, and my body beside, the door while I was with them), I received a long and disturbingly vicious monologue on how evil Sid was, how he'd done nothing for them and how, in spite of all she'd done for him, he was now having an affair. (I could understand him; in circumstances like that, who wouldn't?)

Another time, after a further long harangue on some perceived cause of all their miseries, I brought up the possibility of a psychiatric referral. The response convinced me that mentioning it had not been a good idea and I felt that the small fund of goodwill I'd accumulated had gone into overdraft. As I took my leave that day and the door opened on the normal world, I turned to Louise and remarked that they should really get out a bit on such a lovely day. The response disturbed me.

"She'll *never* go out again!" she said, her eyes narrowing to slits. It was said in the sense of, "I'll make sure she never goes out again," rather than merely as a pessimistic prognosis. It got worse: "If I had something to do it with, I'd kill that Sid — and her" — she nodded in the direction of Millie's room — "then I'd finish myself off too and leave a letter to say I wasn't mad!"

In itself this was not really enough to warrant urgent psychiatric admission (if it were, there'd be more of the population inside than outside), but it made the alarm bells ring even louder than they usually did on these visits. Over the course of the next few visits she was persuaded, after a lot of discussion and cajoling, to accept an appointment (private, at her insistence) with a psychiatrist, although I knew, deep down inside, that the underlying personality disorder would be resistant to any intervention he, or anyone else, could offer.

At least that prediction turned out accurate, but for a long time after the consultation (well, a long time by the standards of our relationship), things were quiet and I was beginning to kid myself that maybe the psychiatrist *had* done some good after all: certainly requests for medication and visits became much less frequent and most of these were dealt with by the others so that for almost a year I had virtually no contact with them.

One morning, towards the end of the surgery, I heard the sound of a fire engine clearing its way as it zoomed past the door of the practice. In those days, and out in the country as we were, emergency vehicles were infrequent enough to raise an eyebrow and a moment of speculation as to the destination; for after all, who was to know that we weren't to become involved, when it was likely that it was heading to somewhere on our patch?

Time passed with no information and the episode was forgotten in the routine of the day. It was early afternoon when the phone rang; this time it was the local Barracks (Police Station to the English reader).

"Sorry to trouble you, Doc . . ." came the voice of one of the constables, one of our patients and well-known to us in both capacities, for he always seemed to be the one who was on duty when we had need of police assistance — suicides, sudden deaths and the like seemed to be becoming his Special Interest, willy-nilly; ". . . but do you have a Louise McNeill, of . . . on your list? We think she might be a patient of yours."

"We do indeed; what has she been up to now?" I replied, wondering what major upheaval had got her out of doors and into the arms of the law.

"Well, now; if we knew that we'd be a whole lot wiser than we are now," came the enigmatic reply. "We were called out to a house fire this morning; there was very extensive damage to the building — I reckon it'll have to come down — but we'd been told there were people in it and once the place was safe, we got in and — well, I'm afraid we found two bodies in one of the bedrooms, both female and both badly charred. We're still trying to locate the third occupant."

"The third occupant is probably out at work," I replied.

"Well let's hope so . . . er . . . you wouldn't happen to know where he works, would you? The next-door occupants are away and there's nobody around to ask."

I passed on the information and sat for a while taking all this in and wondering just what *had* happened there. It could so plausibly have been an accident: after all both of them were often almost insensible from drink, barbiturates, or a combination of both; both smoked liked factory chimneys and spent most of their time in bed. Not too hard, then, to create a picture of what had happened — a lit cigarette, dropped unnoticed onto the bed as they lay senseless, the smoke choking them before they could gather up their fuddled wits to do anything about it. All straightforward — any coroner's court in the land would accept that. But under all this was a nagging darker thought that perhaps things hadn't been just as straightforward as they seemed.

210

What if Louise had carried out her threat and succeeded, if only in two-thirds of her intention? What if she had set the bedroom ablaze and either immolated herself or had been overcome by smoke before she could make, or find, her way out?

There are some questions it's probably better not even to try to answer, if only because no useful purpose would be served by finding out.

Sid was shaken by the event, for after all, there must have been some bond that kept him there (well, most of the time, anyway). Not surprisingly, however, his distress wasn't all that long-lived and his lifestyle soon came to reflect the freedom he'd suddenly acquired, the "affair" blossoming into cohabitation in no time. We saw very little of him after that — after all, he'd seen enough of us to do him a lifetime.

CHAPTER
TWENTY-THREE

Martin

The skies themselves seemed to reflect the mood the day we buried Martin, the black clouds raining torrents down the gullies on the slopes he'd known so well, whose every yard he'd tramped both on and off duty and which looked down on the rain-sodden chapel and graveyard where he was now to lie.

The road was flooded in places and jammed with cars for half a mile in both directions — mere torrential rain wasn't going to put off those to whom he'd been doctor and more for over half a century, those who'd grown old from infancy knowing his care. Professional colleagues, old and not-so-old countrymen — farmers, labourers, mechanics, shop-keepers — all the people who make up a community, crowded into the chapel.

The storms of the preceding few days had wrought havoc in the area and the chapel roof had not been spared: water dripped in onto the pews and the floor, recognisable by little islands of emptiness in a congregation otherwise packed shoulder to shoulder in pews and aisles alike. Unusually in this part of the world, but hardly surprising today, all the denominations of Ulster Christianity were there. As the service got under way, I noted one chap, whose convictions would not normally have brought him within a mile of a Catholic church, slip quietly in at the back to pay his own silent tribute.

My own mind began to wander away from the substance of the Requiem, recalling Martin in his heyday, when I first came to know him. He had a fund of stories from his practice, some of which had involved me as the admitting doctor; it showed just how isolated some people were even then.

"Hello, Hugh." The familiar voice was marginally less welcome at 10p.m. than it might have been in full day, but then he was out and about as well. "You're not going to believe this, but I've just seen an old boy, apparently on my list, for the first time in my life — and if I had seen him, I wouldn't forget it."

"Go on," I said, betraying my interest in the comment.

"Well, he's very sick — I can get no history from him and he's only semi-conscious. He's incontinent of urine and by the smell of him he's been like that for a long time."

"Prostatic?" I queried, knowing that detailed examination in the sort of circumstances he was describing was pretty-nigh impossible.

"Don't think so — now, I haven't examined him in detail; I'm sorry, but it was all I could do to get near him. Odd thing, though; his sister says he's always been wet, as long as she's known him. Anyway, he's almost comatose now; I can't do much for him here."

"OK, I'll sort out a bed and pass you over to Billy for the directions."

Billy was duty driver that night and was really going to love this one. I could hear him already: "Some ould boy at the back o' the mountain — likely never seen soap in his life — we'll all need cleaning down after this . . ." Billy, like all his colleagues, tended to keep his heart of gold under wraps, but it was there in large measure nonetheless.

A couple of hours later, they returned, Billy and his mate in mud-covered Wellingtons and the trolley wheels filthy with mud, soil and the odd bit of grass. Billy was in fine form and greeted me with his Grade One scowl — which meant we would get at least half an hour's craic out of the events.

"Boys-a-dear, thon's a quair fine place ye sent us to — he was two fields over the road. We thought there was a laneway to it, but it ran out in the middle of a field an' I thought we were going to bog down to the axles an' never get out this night." Billy continued, warming to his theme. I'd have preferred to stay, if only to keep him going, but I had to leave to look at his cargo.

A first glance rather confirmed my imagined comments of Billy's; an old man, sallow, unwashed, unshaven for a week or two, making very little attempt to speak — what did come out was barely comprehensible and not informative. "Ah'm wild bad, so Ah am," seemed to be all we were going to get.

The startling thing was not just the strong smell of stale urine — a thing common enough to excite little

214

comment (old men smelling of stale pee are part of the stock in trade of acute medicine) — but the fact that his suit (he was clad, incongruously, in a black suit, with waistcoat and collarless shirt) was rigid and shining with a sort of crystalline lustre, especially the trousers. The nurses and I between us managed to undress him, the girls holding the sodden clothing at arm's length as they consigned it to a plastic bag.

I finally got down to look at his abdomen — and found myself staring at something I'd heard of but never even seen in textbooks: a hole in the abdominal wall, below the navel and in the mid-line, from which urine leaked in a slow trickle.

Here was a case of Ectopia Vesicae — a developmental abnormality where the front of the bladder wall fails to close over and urine, instead of being stored in the bladder, is discharged in a constant dribble to the outside, evaporating to leave its crystalline residue on skin or clothing.

The astonishing thing was that this was not a newborn baby, but a man in his seventies at least, whose problem would have been immediately apparent at birth. He had lived all his life like this, unknown to schools, doctors, district nurses or anyone. I could only ponder why. Perhaps the circumstances of his birth (or more likely conception) had been a cause for shame and the affliction seen as a punishment for a misdeed, real or imagined. It was hard to conceive of the life he must have led — seemingly only his sister had known of his existence and had not betrayed it until now, when his situation had gone beyond even her ability to cope.

I rang Martin the next day, telling him the story.

"Funny, you know," he said. "I'd have seen the sister now and again, but she never asked for a call — always came to the surgery. Never mentioned anyone else. Strange, isn't it?"

Next day, Martin rang in. "Thought you might like to know we seem to have no record of him at all, although his sister's adamant that he's one of mine. How is he today, then?"

"Poorly — he's in terminal renal failure and I reckon he's not going to last much longer."

And he didn't — his extraordinary, miserable, isolated existence came to an end only two or three days later. I can't help wondering what sort of person he might have been had someone known of his existence — even when he was born, in the last quarter of the nineteenth century, he could have had some sort of repair and had his life transformed.

We'll never know.

The service went on, the words barely audible from where we were, jammed in at the back of the chapel, for the storm had put paid to the loudspeaker system. It seemed to have done for the central heating as well and we had to wait for the body mass of the congregation to raise a bit of heat, causing sodden old overcoats to steam gently. With that came the smell — not of incense but of old garments long immured in foisty farmhouse bedroom wardrobes, coming out only on special occasions. Old dampness mingling with even older sweat and the occasional waft of mothballs made a not-altogether-incongruous mix, for these were his people — he'd seen the sweat, the grime and the toil that made it; it was as much a part of his life as of theirs.

I could just see, across the nave, glimpses of the hills — he'd have known every gully, every sapling growing in them in his walks, walks in the course of which he'd worn out two natural and about six artificial hips. "Ah, now," he once said, "there's none of 'em'll stand up to twenty miles a day!" Not a man to let mere trivia like a set of hip replacements slow him down.

". . . and let Light Perpetual shine upon him . . ." We shuffled a bit, snuffled and coughed a bit and tried to hear what was being said. But the memories kept on intruding — and why not? Funerals are a time for memories as much as ritual.

It wasn't that Martin had a monopoly on isolated patients, but when your practice extends miles into the mountains, with a few isolated farms and even fewer and more isolated cottages the only human habitations, then you're bound to collect a few oddities whose lives have been untrammelled by much contact with their fellow human beings. One heard of dark doings with sheep but I suspect these were stories put about by the village-dwellers to demonstrate their urban superiority — even if most of them hadn't ever been to the nearest town, nine miles away.

One story of Martin's illustrated, again, the extremes of rural life and eventually provided one of our surgeons with a story to dine out on among the urban sophisticates of Belfast and even London.

One of the most isolated farms — if you can call a once-thatched, now-corrugated-iron-covered shack, a few even more decrepit outhouses and a few acres of sodden rough pasture a farm — was occupied by an ageing brother and sister who scraped some sort of living from a few cattle, hens around the yard and not much else.

Martin's visits were infrequent — only once or twice a year at most, for they were hardy people who didn't trouble doctors or anyone else unless they really needed to: still, he knew the way there without needing directions.

Once, as he turned into the squalid little area that the hens usually claimed as theirs, he caught sight of a figure disappearing into one of the outhouses; the glimpse was so brief he wasn't even sure that he'd seen anything, but the impression of a movement persisted. A casual question about anyone else in the house (although he felt the very concept of visitors was strange to them) elicited a definite negative and he didn't press the point — maybe he had been mistaken.

A year or so later, however, the scene was replayed and this time there was no mistaking her: a middle-aged woman who hid herself not quite quickly enough to avoid being seen.

Gentle questioning (I would imagine spread over a few visits) revealed the woman to be the daughter of the brother and sister. "Hardly to be wondered at," he

218

commented. "Long cold nights and no company — only surprise is that they've kept her hidden so long."

This poor creature, bereft of any care or human contact other than from her parents, and wholly devoid of education, was in addition significantly mentally handicapped, though how much was congenital handicap and how much the result of gross deprivation was never really sorted out. She had been trained to hide if ever anyone approached the place — something she'd obviously been good at, for no-one prior to this knew of her existence and the secret shame of her conception had remained just that, secret from all the World.

Time passed and the hardy old couple went the way of all hardy old couples, leaving "The Girl" her inheritance; poor and squalid as it was, it was indisputably her own, for there was no living soul around or related to dispute it. She managed to eke out an existence, seeing few and trusting fewer, as the years went by.

She was well past middle age when she developed symptoms that really couldn't be ignored and needed investigation. Martin had kept an eye on her and was one of the trusted ones, but even he had difficulty persuading her to go down to the hospital — in an ambulance! Poor soul, she had never been in a vehicle before, had never seen the village, let alone the town — and as for meeting all those strangers . . . It was like being sent to the Moon.

The surgeon, a good and wise man who knew the ways of the area, had been well primed and in the event the consultation had gone off extremely well, so well in fact that she readily agreed to come back for a follow-up visit. This time her gratitude found tangible expression in the form of a small sack which she carried into the clinic. The nurses went to take it while she got undressed, but she wouldn't let it go so it went into the cubicle with her.

Sister went into the cubicle with the surgeon; by now everyone knew her story, one way or another, and took more than a professional interest in her wellbeing.

"Doctor, I've brought you a wee something."

"Ach, that's very kind of you, Nellie, but there's no need for it, you know."

"Ah, but ye're all so good to me — here y'are" . . . whereupon she opened the sack.

The contents hadn't been expecting this and had not been properly secured; out of the sack like a little cannonball came a very cross cockerel, alive and in fine fighting trim.

In seconds mayhem descended on the place, as the bird, avoiding well-meaning but clumsy attempts on its liberty, perched on cubicle partitions, window ledges, taps and anything it could even try to get a grip on. Other patients, half-naked in adjoining cubicles, reacted with screams and shrieks to the creature's appearance above them, for the cubicles were all open-topped and afforded easy transit for a bird while making it virtually impossible for anyone earthbound and constrained by such things as doors and curtains to get even close to it. Even worse for the hapless onlookers, every time it came near being caught and flew off, it did what birds often do and shat copiously on whatever was below it. The scene — patients screaming and waving wildly, while nurses tried to hunt down a noisy and incontinent cockerel — is best left to the imagination; even some of the "good-living" staff found words no one realised they knew. By the time the bird was recaptured and order restored there was little of the morning left. I'd be sure that the story was all over the area by the afternoon — after all, it's not every visitor to Out-patients who can come away with a tale like that.

And Nellie? Well, you see, there are no funny stories in Medicine: investigations revealed a well-advanced malignancy (I don't know where and it doesn't matter). She went downhill very quickly, spending her last weeks in the wards, with more material comfort and human fellowship than she'd ever known.

What became of her bit of land I never knew: I suspect that one of the trusted few took it for its bit of mean pasture and used the buildings for storing hay, the boundary between it and the adjoining ground blurring, then disappearing altogether, just as she had done.

The rain eased for us as we committed "Earth to Earth . . . Dust to Dust". Even if it hadn't, there'd have been no hurrying of this, the last Rite of Passage. Then slowly, in twos and threes, talking low, the crowd began to break up and move away. Martin was gone, "full of years and honour". Can any of us ask more?

CHAPTER
TWENTY-FOUR

Memories

I knew, as soon as I looked out of the window that morning, what sort of problems the day was going to bring me. The ice lay thick on the ground, showing that even in Ulster the rain can sometimes freeze. Ice always takes the Ulsterman by surprise and those who are not sliding cars all over the roads and making violent contact with other cars (or more immovable objects) go out of their front doors and immediately lose their footing on this wholly foreign material.

Many of the elderly living far out in the country up in the hills see this sort of weather more often than we "townies" do and, while they fall just as often, tend to be rather more fatalistic about it. A fall on the wrist will be ignored for the first day ("Ach, sure, it's nought but a wee hurt"); when the swelling increases and the pain persists into the next day a little more notice is taken of it ("My, but thon's still brave and sore!"); by the next day it's becoming, if anything, more disabling ("Mebbie I should get that looked at"); persistence into the next day confirms the idea and they make their way to the GP, who diagnoses the fracture at a glance and refers them on to Casualty.

222

Thus it is that many upland dwellers present themselves three days later with a grossly swollen, bruised and almost immobile wrist. The question "When did this happen?" was always asked, but you knew the answer in advance ("Ach now, it was a whean o' days ago, when thon bad frost was on the ground, ye mind.').

So, today would be a Road Accident Day with a few of the more promptly presenting fractures thrown in. All time-consuming stuff, but the counterbalance was that most of those with trivial problems would be sufficiently put off to stay at home, or a least to venture no further than the nearest pub.

Sure enough, by late morning we had assembled two or three wrist fractures, to be manipulated once we'd cleared the victims of a couple of, fortunately, not-too-severe RTAs. At that time these injuries, known as Colles' fractures, were usually set under a general anaesthetic as the other methods then available gave poorer pain relief. (Things are different now and in most centres one or other form of local anaesthetic is the preferred option.)

The last of these was a lady in, I suppose, her sixties, with a classical Colles' which she hadn't kept to herself for three days, but had made her own accurate diagnosis and come straight down to us. As I spoke to her I felt that I'd seen her somewhere before, but after thirty-odd years in one smallish place that was hardly surprising. The name was a common one in the area she came from and there was nothing in the case notes to indicate that I'd ever treated her in the past; still, there was that "I've seen you before" feeling and I suspected that it was reciprocated, by the way she looked at me once or twice.

The procedure was straightforward once the anaesthetist had her nicely unconscious and it was only a few minutes before the cast was on the wrist and the gas could be turned off. A short job like this allowed a rapid recovery and we were tidying up as she came round. Short-lived confusion during recovery is not at all unusual, but as she came up into that half-world between the unconscious and the fully alert she began to weep loudly; then, with a sorrow and bitterness that seemed to come from the very depths of her being, she cried out, "Seamus, Seamus, oh my Seamus!" The tears streamed down her cheeks as she slid back into a sleep.

Then the pieces fell into place, a quarter of a century slipped away and I knew.

It was just another normal day (if any day in an emergency unit can ever be called "normal"). I had been in the job only a year or two and was still finding my feet in the subtleties of a speciality still without a structure or training programme, although I'd learned very early on that the unexpected was the rule in this sort of work. So it was with no more than the usual squirt of adrenaline that I took the call from switchboard: "Ambulance is just on its way out to an RTA — they'll radio back when they've more information."

I made ready our meagre resources — two tiny cubicles and a bare area, where plasters were applied, were always inadequate for multiple casualties, so first call was to the operating theatre which was closely adjacent to us and doubled up as resuscitation area (though they were never called such in those days). It was crowded, as it always was in mid-afternoon. I told the surgeon of the situation as far as I knew it.

"Right — I've only a couple of hernias left to do now, so we can hold off starting them until we know more, eh?" He'd been around a long time and knew, as I had already learned, that 999 calls could encompass anything from the moribund with multiple injuries to those who had got up and gone away after the call had been made; so apart from alerting those who needed to know, further action could wait until we had some idea of what was coming.

The RTA was only about five miles away so we didn't have long to wait; the receptionist worked the phones and relayed radio messages from the receiver and transmitter on her desk — state of the art technology at the time. There was concern and anxiety in her voice, for in this part of the world "no man is an island" indeed, and she could well find that she knew the victims.

"Billy's just off the radio — reception's so bad I can hardly make him out but I think he has two with him, both very bad. They're having to work on them before they dare set off." (When you recall that at that time the only qualifications required of an ambulance driver were a clean driving licence and a First-Aid Certificate

— probably with more emphasis on the former — you realise what heroes these fellows were: often tackling complex situations well beyond their level of formal training, they always delivered the goods in a way that they, and we, could be proud of.)

I knew things were bad by the looks on the crew's faces as they brought the first one in on the trolley and a glance at their cargo confirmed it. A young man — at least we thought he was, for his face was so damaged that even that was less than certain — his breathing irregular, chest movements all wrong (multiple rib fractures with complications) and an abdomen swollen and tense all pointed to major multiple internal injuries.

The first hernia was returned to the ward, his operation postponed at least until much later in the day while attention was directed entirely to this, the latest of a constant flow of unfortunates — for at this time in Ireland not only were there no seat belts, airbags or padded steering wheels (I'm not sure if even racing cars had seat belts then) but there was no driving test, no speed limits, no MOT and no means of measuring blood alcohol. Days of innocence they may have been, but the price in carnage (gross and spectacular as it often was) was paid out every day by someone.

It soon became apparent that we were fighting a losing battle this time; uncontrollable bleeding from within both abdomen and chest led inevitably to a cardiac arrest (even today, cardiac arrest in those circumstances is almost always fatal: at that time he stood no chance, despite all our efforts). We looked at each other, the surgeon, the anaesthetist, myself.

"I think we may as well give up now," said the anaesthetist, himself not a man to throw in the towel lightly. The voice expressed the sense of defeat we all felt.

"Are any of his family here yet?" asked the surgeon.

"Don't know — in fact I haven't even got a name for him yet, although I imagine the nurses will have found out by now. I don't think Billy had much of a chance to go namehunting at the scene, anyway," I replied.

I cleaned myself up and went back to the Department.

"How's the other bloke?" I asked.

"Oh, he's not as bad as we'd thought," said Sister, "Dr McWilliams is with him, but there's nothing too urgent about him, I think. Your other man didn't make it, then?"

"'fraid not — just too much, too badly damaged. Did you ever get a name for him yet, by the way?"

"Not for sure — there's no identification on him — but there's been two or three calls enquiring about a Seamus Bradley from an RTA in the same area. Your other man's still badly concussed and can't tell us anything yet."

It was over an hour later that two RUC officers arrived, accompanied by a frightened-looking woman in her early forties, a coat thrown on over whatever she had been wearing when the knock came to her door.

One of the policemen stepped onto the office; he spoke in a low voice to avoid being overheard by his charge.

"We've a Mrs Bradley here; we think it may be her son who's been involved in that RTA this afternoon. Would you have names for the occupants?"

I explained the situation to him. He was a young man and was visibly taken aback at the news.

"I'll talk to her," I said, "'though God knows just what I'm going to say to her."

Breaking news of this sort is always a testing experience for the one doing so, but in a situation like this, "breaking it gently" is almost impossible. There wasn't much doubt about the identity; she described his clothing in detail (I couldn't bring myself to ask about his face, having seen what havoc had been wrought on it). As slowly as I could I let her come to realise that her son, who'd gone out a couple of hours before on some banal errand on a banal afternoon, was not coming back and her life would never be the same again. She took it with outward calmness, although the rigid face hid only some of her feelings. She murmured something about it being "God's will" and asked to see him. By then the girls had got him cleaned up and made as presentable as you can make a smashed-up face. Someone would have to make a formal identification anyway, so we took her in to see her son as she would never have wished to see him.

"Aye, that's him, so it is," she said softly.

We let her stay with him for a while, the girls keeping a discreet eye on her from a distance, until she turned away and moved to the door. We knew her husband was on his way over from work and it wasn't long before he joined her. They didn't stay long after that, but as they left she turned and said, "Thank you, doctor — I know you did your best." In that moment I shared the sense of sorrow that far transcends the sadness of failure and, young as I was then, wondered if I would ever have the same dignity as they had showed in that situation.

I said something about "some things being just too much for anyone to cope with", realising as I said it how it applied to both of us in its different ways. I walked with them to the door and watched them go away to grieve.

She was nicely on the trolley in the recovery area, sleeping off the anaesthetic. The anaesthetist and I washed our hands and made for the kettle in the theatre ante-room, for it looked as if a cup of basic-grade instant coffee each was going to have to do for lunch — the waiting room was starting to fill up for the afternoon and a surgical list awaited him in about ten minutes' time.

"Wonder what all the 'Seamus, Seamus' — ing was all about," he said.

"I know what it was," I replied. I told him the story of the tragedy twenty-five years earlier.

"You know," I went on, "I wonder if she ever really let her feelings go and had a good angry, grief-stricken scream at life; perhaps it's only in a situation like this that the emotion breaks through."

229

"... Or perhaps when the house is still at night and the memory rises again as a nightmare," he said thoughtfully.

"Perhaps — but I won't ask her," I said, "It doesn't always do to be stirring up old ghosts and re-opening old wounds, does it?"

CHAPTER
TWENTY-FIVE

Drumlargan

There are very few houses which have about them so over-whelming a sense of gloom as Drumlargan; I think it's the only place which has ever literally made my spine tingle — and it never fails in this, day or night.

As it happened my first visit there was at night, just my luck. I had been well primed about the set-up there — the drunken, bone-idle father who, in between beating his wife, had produced half a dozen or so children. To their credit, the daughters had cleared off to the city as soon as they were old enough, or could pass as old enough, leaving the father to slide down the alcoholic slope and the sons to build up an unpalatable reputation for violence, violence which they inflicted on each other and on the Old Man (who, being their father, no doubt gave as good as he got). Of late the father had taken, not to his bed, but to his chair, not leaving it even to empty bowels or bladder: the state in which he existed is better left to the imagination, especially considering the level of care offered by his belligerent and often hostile offspring. (His wife, long ago worn out by battering, child-bearing and the depression that comes from all of that, had decamped for a better life one morning and hadn't been heard of since — it was probably the wisest move of her whole life.)

The night call had been to the old man. I always thought of him as the Old Man; although he was little over sixty, the years and his lifestyle had not dealt kindly with him. In spite of the directions given to me I almost missed the turning off the little country road onto the cart track that led to the house. A couple of hundred yards of mud and boulders that might have accommodated a tractor with some ease, but made heavy going for a small saloon, brought into view the dark grey forbidding silhouette of a house, half-hidden by a clump of tall trees through whose tops a full moon shone, accentuating the eeriness of its blind, unlit windows. I stopped and got out, but as I walked over to it I realised the place was empty, for not only was it in darkness, there was no door to it — only an opening, through which I could just make out bales of hay stacked in what had been the hall. Then I remembered something in the directions given over the phone: "Past the first house," they'd said. I must have taken the wrong lane, but in that respect the directions had been quite unequivocal.

Scouting around in the light of the moon and the car headlamps I found that the track wound round the house and into the copse. I set off to follow it, finding the surface change from the merely bad to the appalling. At least I could reverse out of it if I was wrong, but the track went through the wood and after a few dozen yards opened out before another grim grey house. The solitary oil lamp in the window enhanced rather than relieved the weird spooky air of the place and the bright moon casting onto the wall the shadows of the tree tops did nothing to make it less so.

My confident knock (a doctor's knock has to be confident, however hopeless the problem he faces) was answered almost immediately by a teenager who looked as if he'd just come in from shifting a ton of manure with his bare hands — and smelt accordingly. No word was spoken but he offered me a thoroughly unwholesome leer, which I took to be a gesture of welcome. He nodded his head over to what had been the kitchen, in the days when the house was better organised.

The Old Man was sitting in his chair surrounded by empty beer bottles and a stench of urine, excrement and stale alcohol that made a real olfactory breath-catcher. Only his eyes moved in recognition of my entry.

Around him, arranged like a bodyguard around a throne, stood the sons of the house, dressed much as the one who'd let me in and all as silent and as menacing.

"Well, now, what's the trouble?" I said, with a heartiness belied by my restless glancing at the bodyguards.

"It's me bowels," the old man muttered, almost without moving his lips. "They're all stopped up."

"Thank God for that," I thought, although the odour around him gave the lie to his complaint. A few further questions confirmed what was already apparent — his diet consisted largely of alcohol, from which he got the few calories he needed for his vegetative existence, plus an odd slice of bread and margarine on the rare occasions when he felt ravenously hungry. His "constipation", though little wonder, was an unalloyed blessing in the circumstances.

I explained the reason for his problem as briefly as I could: I had no wish to make a conversation of it and reckoned he was as poor a candidate as you could find for dietary re-education. He smiled, or came as near to a smile as I suppose he ever did.

"Will ye take a wee drink afore ye go, Doctor?" he said. This was fulsome hospitality indeed; he fished for an unopened bottle among the pile at his feet. Hastily I insisted that I never took a drink when on duty; as I never normally do, I could look him straight in the eye when saying so and he took me at my word, putting down the bottle he'd just found and noting its position, for retrieval as soon as my back was turned.

I said goodnight and left as rapidly as decorum would allow — I still had the feeling that one wrong word would see my throat cut on the spot. The heavy front door closed immediately I'd passed though it and I stepped over the grass-covered forecourt and into the car without a backward glance, although I was sure that I was being watched from the windows.

The car felt almost like home as I closed the door, started up, turned round and put on the radio as I crawled back down the track into the copse. Over the air came the sounds of the Mozart Clarinet Quintet, and I wondered for a moment if there could be any

234

greater distance in the world between that and where I'd just been. Lulled by the music, I was nearly halfway home before I remembered I hadn't delivered my usual rebuke to those who make unjustified night calls. On reflection, however, I felt that some things, sometimes, were better left unsaid.

The old man lasted an incredibly long time in that state; I saw him rarely, for despite the unnecessary night call, he made few demands on us. My failure to examine him more fully that night turned out to be of no consequence for as far as I ever heard his bowels continued in their usual way; then he began to lose weight and his smoker's cough became steadily worse. We managed to prise him from his chair — almost literally, as it were — and got him as far as the local X-ray department. The pictures only confirmed what we had already guessed — a huge mass of lung cancer filling one side of his chest and already widespread, far beyond definitive treatment. We did what little there was to be done, even managing to get him to the regional radiotherapy centre for some palliation. I suppose that once he did get out of his chair, the rest of any trip was easy, although he was soon in no condition to notice where he was going.

On one of these last visits, the door was opened to me by a youngish, well-dressed and very personable woman, whose accent and vocabulary made me assume she was a visiting social or voluntary worker. My non-committal conversation was rewarded by learning that this was one of the daughters, long departed from the family home. She apologised for the house, for her brothers, for her father most of all, as she smiled, shrugged her shoulders and said softly, "You see how it is with him, how it's been for years. Betty and me, we got out of it, but the boys are too much like their father — they'll all go the same way as time goes on, y'know."

Sadly, I think she's going to be proved right.

CHAPTER
TWENTY-SIX

The Patio

The Moores lived at the limit of our catchment and although they were barely a hundred yards from the main road they could have been ten miles from it for all you'd have seen of the place as you drove along. Surprisingly, I'd been in the practice for several years before I even heard of them; I imagine they'd always regarded J as Their Doctor and myself as a mere *parvenu*, to be called upon only if needs must.

J overheard me asking directions from our receptionist one day, when presumably Needs *did* Must. "Aha," he said, his eyes full of fun, "the Patio."

"The Patio?"

"Aye, the Patio, me boy."

I waited, reflecting his grin — a story was obviously brewing.

"If you go out through Ballyrath on the main road, just before you come to the phone box, there's a wee lane in to the right and at the end of that lane lies The Patio, a splendid detached residence for two." He went on to explain how the two in question, old bachelor brothers (a third had long predeceased them) had lived in a traditional long single-storey Ulster farmhouse which had gradually fallen into decay. First the byre adjoining it, together with the little washroom-cum-store, had lost their turf roofs as the old rotten timbers gave way, then the process had extended inexorably to involve the living quarters, causing first the kitchen then the living room roofs to follow suit, until eventually the only covered part of the house was the small bedroom at the end of the house furthest from the byre.

The brothers' response to this was of the simplest — as each section collapsed they just took to managing in what was left and now lived a rather cramped existence in what had become, by default, a bed-sitter.

It was a glorious summer's day as I turned into the laneway — to say it was lined with trees would suggest a degree of planning unknown to the disordered hedgerow and its taller elements. I passed a pile of sand, looking weathered as if it had been there since the autumn before, together with a stack of dirty bricks stacked against what might once have been the wheel of a horse-drawn hay rake. Over a patch of grass and baked earth behind the house, a length of baler twine carried the week's washing — dirt-greyed long woollen combinations and a pair or two of equally grubby socks. If this was the clean end, I wondered, what they had been like to start with?

The house was as J had described it, only more so; the roofless parts lacked doors and windows as well, and at first sight it was hard to see just how one reached the lived-in bit.

No one stirred but in the silence I felt sure that the noise of the car's approach would have been heard. I stepped through the rubble-strewn opening that had been the kitchen door and worked my way across the area. The door beyond this was intact and closed; as I went towards it I realised I was on an even floor of large clay tiles, the sun shining down on them. Of course — the Patio! I tried not to laugh aloud, but rattled at the door knob (it was really an internal door and lacked such things as lock and knocker — which would have been wholly irrelevant anyway). I thought I heard some half-coherent sound from inside and took it to mean, "Come in," so I did.

It was like entering a broom cupboard or one of those "glory holes" that every established family has somewhere in their house, where all the assorted rubbish which might one day "come in handy" is consigned to perpetual gloom. At first I could see nothing — the tiny window, covered by a filthy piece of net curtain, let in hardly any light. I was jammed between the edge of the door and a huge tallboy chest of drawers, its varnish jet-black. A tiny table under the window held some grubby crockery, a jar or two, a tin teapot and, incongruously, a plastic bottle of detergent. Two wooden chairs were unoccupied. Another second's glance showed an old fireplace at the far end, faced by a settee whose brown cover had given way in several places. This too was empty.

"Are you the doctor?" came the half-coherent mutter again, from the still-impenetrable gloom beside me. I looked round. Squeezed into the space between the back of the tallboy and the wall was a double bed, the first two feet or so of which projected out beyond the former, the rest being lost in the pitch blackness behind it. Not to this day have I seen the foot of that bed and I doubt if its occupants ever did, either.

George was in bed. At least he was on the side nearest to me, for which I was grateful; had he been on the other side I would have had to climb into bed with him to examine him and I felt that the state of the bedsheets suggested we'd have plenty of company. George, being significantly the elder, had some "trouble with the water", so slept on the outside to have ready access to the bucket against which I banged my shin as I homed in on him. Jim had a choice of entry and exit — either he climbed over George or he climbed over the settee back which butted against the bed head. Either route offered a challenge to an arthritic septuagenarian like Jim.

George lay, grey in hair and countenance under his layers of grime; he was over eighty and, as the locals would say, "the years were there". I made little conversation with him, for he could barely hear me shout and was obviously in a degree of heart failure — not a new problem, as I had learned before coming out to him. By dint of coaxing and pushing I was able to examine the back of his chest and his lower back for signs of fluid accumulation. The challenge of finding and examining his feet, tucked away in the distant darkness, was one I unhesitatingly funked, for that could have added half an hour to the visit on its own by the time the status quo was restored. I settled for a bellowed, "Feet alright?" and took the affirmative nod as diagnostic.

I was about to start sorting out his medicines when the door was pushed open and brother Jim came in, tall and quite sprightly, if a bit stiff around the knees, as he placed a little loaded shopping bag on the table, shunting things around to make a space for it.

"Well, now, Doctor, how is he?"

I said he'd really need some different tablets as the ones he had didn't seem to be helping him.

"Right then, you give me the 'scription then and I'll nip into town for it now."

"How will you go?" I asked. I'd heard no car and, frankly, Jim didn't look the car-owning type. His face, grimy as his brother's, took on a fleeting grin as he replied, "Oh, I'll just take a run up on the bike." He'd just come from there, five none-too-level miles away; no wonder he was a bit stiff as he came in!

We stepped outside and I made for the car. "I see you're going to do a bit of building," I said, tactfully refraining from adding, "and high time too."

"Doctor," said Jim, laying a confidential hand on my arm as he warmed to his subject, "I'm going to build a nice modern wee bungalow here and clear all this away." He waved at the house. "You can't go on living in a place like that now, can you?"

I concurred politely (and fervently under my breath). "But just you wait and see, Doctor; it'll be a grand wee place, for there's a great view and it's quiet and peaceful even though we're so close to the road." His voice dropped, became confiding. "This might not look much to you, Doc, but it's Heaven and Earth to me."

I looked round, over the low plain, green with high summer, and beyond to the heat-hazed distance where the hills rose out of it fifteen or more miles away. Only birdsong disturbed the silence as the sun beat down on us.

I could see his point.

"Well, what was the Patio like today?" said J when we met up again. "And how's George?"

I duly reported the story and said brightly, "But I see Jim's going to build a new bungalow on the site — he's got the bricks in already."

J smiled slowly, his eyes focused far away. "Man dear, that pile of bricks was delivered near-on twenty-five years ago; the sand washes away but every now and again Jim brings in another load — that way he can go on dreaming."

While they were regular users of the service by day, to give them their due we rarely heard from them out of hours. Thus it was with some concern that I heard Jim's voice on the phone one night just after midnight: it had the softness and clarity that so often characterises the real emergency.

"Doctor, will you come and see George?"

"What's the trouble?"

"I think he's dying, Doctor."

"I'll be right there."

Out along the main road, I slowed down to search for the lane end, then drove up the hundred yards or so of pitch darkness to the house. The door opened to greet me and the light of a gas lantern flickered over the Patio.

George lay very much as I had first met him: he had been dead for at least ten or fifteen minutes and no medical knowledge was needed to confirm the fact.

Jim stood holding the gas lantern high to let its light diffuse into the corners. "I doubt he's gone to his rest, Doctor," he said softly. The lantern was close enough to his face to show the red rimming his eyes.

"Aye, Jim, I don't think I can do anything for him now." I laid a hand on his arm, more instinctively than premeditatedly. "Can I do anything for you? It's very late."

"No, no, Doctor. I'll need to get some place to wake him though, for there's no room in here, so there's not."

At that moment I felt more sorrow than I had known for a long time. Here was an old man, his even older brother a corpse in the bed they shared, in a space which couldn't physically admit a coffin, let alone place it with any dignity or accommodate friends and relatives for a wake.

As we pondered this, a car came round the gable and stopped. A young man, a stranger to me, but obviously well-acquainted with the brothers, entered without formality. He glanced at me and I shook my head almost imperceptibly; no more was needed.

"My sorrow for your troubles, Jim," said the stranger, taking his hand. We explained the problem — an all-too-apparent one — and to my relief the young man took charge. "I'll run down town and see Bobby (the local undertaker); he'll sort things out, for he has a nice wee parlour, I think."

I felt I could now leave with a clear conscience and said my goodnights. Jim accompanied me to the car as we exchanged a few banal comments. As I put my hand on the door handle I looked up over the car roof: the plain lay in a darkness dotted by the few lights still burning so late, but, just clear of the skyline, a crescent moon illuminated the backdrop to the black ridge of the hills. We both fell momentarily silent and still, then I quietly got in and drove slowly away.

Heaven and Earth, indeed.

Also available in ISIS Large Print:

Wigan Pier Goodbye

Ted Dakin

"My escape from a school that taught me very little was a euphoric occasion and because of the headmaster's ruling that only short pants should be worn by all pupils, my first pair of long ones was an added bonus."

Ted Dakin returns to his childhood in Wigan, with more stories of the people and places he grew up with. He tells of boxing matches ruled over by his vindictive headmaster, Owd Hector Wainwright; of men stealing coal from the trains; and of his first job in a saddlery. Full of the characters of his youth, like Dolly Varden and her predictions, Fag-Ash Lil and Dunkirk veteran Ginger Dyson, Ted's stories are full of the warmth and wit of a Wigan lad.

ISBN 978-0-7531-9510-9 (hb)
ISBN 978-0-7531-9511-6 (pb)

Charismatic Cows and Beefcake Bulls

Sonia Kurta

"Brownie was always prepared to challenge any cow who she didn't recognise as being part of her herd. Unfortunately this included herself and, on seeing her reflection in the plate glass windows of shops we passed, she would lower her head and prepare to charge."

Cows staging protests, puzzle-solving geese and a rebellious mopper-upper - these are just a few of the engaging characters who Sonia Kurta met during her time in farming. And that's not to mention the farm workers in every shape and size or the occasional boss who just had to be kept in his place.

Based largely in Cornwall, Sonia gathered experience on farms ranging in size from one-horse establishments to the great Caerhays estate. These lively and accurate recollections show the fun that was to be had in the last days of the working horse.

ISBN 978-0-7531-9508-6 (hb)
ISBN 978-0-7531-9509-3 (pb)